W9-BUX-622

PHOTO BY BRADY

PHOTO BY BRADY

A PICTURE OF THE CIVIL WAR

JENNIFER ARMSTRONG

Atheneum Books for Young Readers

NEW YORK • LONDON • TORONTO • SYDNEY

ATHENEUM BOOKS FOR YOUNG READERS

An imprint of Simon & Schuster Children's Publishing Division

1230 Avenue of the Americas, New York, New York 10020

Copyright © 2005 by Jennifer Armstrong

Book design by Nina Miller Design

The text for this book is set in Ehrhardt MT and Grotesque MT.

Manufactured in the United States of America

First Edition

10 9 8 7 6 5 4 3 2 1

Library of Congress Cataloging-in-Publication Data

Armstrong, Jennifer, 1961–

Photo by Brady : a picture of the Civil War / Jennifer Armstrong.— 1st ed.

p. cm.

Includes bibliographical references.

ISBN 0-689-85785-3

1. United States—History—Civil War, 1861–1865—Juvenile literature. 2. Brady, Mathew B., 1823 (ca.)–1896—Juvenile literature. 3. Photographers—United States—Biography—Juvenile literature. 4. United States—History—Civil War, 1861–1865—Photography—Juvenile literature. I. Brady, Mathew B., 1823 (ca.)–1896. II. Title.

E468.A756 2004

973.7'3'0222–dc22   2004008967

For my group: Alex, Bruce, Joe, Karen, and Patrice. I owe you many thanks.

ACKNOWLEDGMENTS

The hard work of many historians paved the road for me. For their years of scholarship on Mathew Brady and Civil War photography, I tip my hat to Mary Panzer and William A. Frassanito. For Civil War history, I think none can beat Bruce Catton for readability and humanity. The many scholars who have labored to edit and compile diaries and letters have done all of us an invaluable service, giving us the voices of the men and women who fought in and witnessed the Civil War, and to them I owe many thanks. Thank you also to my patient editor, Julia Richardson, for trusting me. Lastly, my friend Emma Dodge Hanson has taught me that in photography, it's all about the frame: what you leave in, and what you leave out.

AUTHOR'S NOTE

With this report of the Civil War I have focused almost exclusively on the struggle as it played out in Virginia and the East, and on the activities of the Union Army of the Potomac, President Lincoln, and the photographers based in New York City and Washington. It is by no means a complete picture, and is possibly unbalanced, but every photographer has to leave something outside the frame. I have also taken, without apology, the side of the Union.

CONTENTS

Collodion
Preparation of the Plate

Exposure

Developing the Image

Fixing the Image

Notes
Bibliography
Picture Credits
Index

PHOTO BY BRADY

COLLODION

Collodion:

A highly flammable, colorless or yellowish syrupy solution of pyroxylin, ether, and alcohol, used as an adhesive to close small wounds and hold surgical dressings, in topical medications, and for making photographic plates.

Imagine you are walking across a field the morning after a battle. The ground is littered with cast-aside haversacks, muskets whose wooden stocks have been shattered by gunfire, forage caps, ramrods, the crumpled paper of used cartridges, a pocket Testament trampled into the mud. With the toe of your boot you turn over the little book; then, squatting, you trace the lines of the stained page with one finger: *but whosoever shall smite thee on thy right cheek, turn to him the other also.*

Which man was it who grasped this text in one hand while digging in his cartridge box with the other? That man there, his dead eyes staring at the sky? Both of his cheeks are black with gunpowder, from the frenzy of biting off the ends of the cartridges and tipping the powder down the barrel of his musket.

And as your gaze travels past him, you take in the slow and sober activity of the ground: the regimental musicians, having laid aside their drums and bugles, are now gathering the dead, laying the corpses in rows as if in battle formation. This is a farmer's field, you realize, and there at the edge of the clearing is the farmer's house. A red flag hangs from an upper window to identify it as a field hospital.

Yesterday, as the battle was waged, you waited in the rear with the supply trains. But even at a distance it was obvious how quickly the air thickened with smoke, like a thundercloud lit by lightning flashes of artillery. You noticed how grapeshot hitting the trees sounded like a fistful of pebbles hitting the side of a barn, and how the rapid fire of muskets recalled to your memory your mother tearing old calico into strips for bandages. Some bullets sounded like nothing so much as the strike of a buggy whip across a broad cabbage leaf; some screeched like a cat whose tail is trodden on. Tomorrow this engagement will be known in the papers by the name of the nearest town, or the nearest creek or courthouse. The Federals favor creek names for battles—Bull Run, Antietam; the Rebels name them for towns—Manassas, Sharpsburg.

But today, today the armies are preparing to move on, to another field by another wood and another farmer's house. Today falls to you the task of photographing this field. You are one of Brady's operators, and over there by that wrecked artillery piece is your darkroom on wheels, and the mule that pulls it is whisking his tail at carrion flies. In the wagon are the bottles of collodion and silver nitrate, the racks of fragile glass plates, the heavy box camera on its tripod. Mr. Brady has mortgaged his successful New York studio to supply you with this equipment, has gotten permission from Father Abraham himself to photograph this war, because it must be recorded. It must be captured in pictures. Where will you set up the camera? How will you record what happened here? How will you show to the people back home what terror existed on this field yesterday—the smell, the death screams, the generals gnawing their cigars to cud as they tried to follow the movement of regimental flags through the smoke with their field glasses? How will you know if your picture shows more than just the grisly aftermath of battle, silent and still?

This will be hard, this will be even more of a challenge than usual. There are so many pictures that you can't take—the exposure time for wet-plate photographs is so long, longer than it takes to say "Ready, aim, fire," longer than it takes an artillery crew to load another ten-pound shot into a sizzling-hot gun, longer than it takes an ambulance crew to hoist a man onto a stretcher. So many pictures you can't take because there is no water at all anywhere near for washing the exposed plates, or because the light is too dim, or because your mule bolted and ran away with the wagon, breaking all the glass negatives and the unexposed plates with them. So many pictures you can't take because—because how do you show that man who is crying over his killed son, that farmwife whose kitchen table is covered with the gore of amputations, that ragtag army of runaway slaves who are following the Federals and whispering "*Jubilee*"?

But now the photograph must be made, because your job is to show not just the facts of this Civil War but its meaning. If that means rearranging this dead boy so—place his hand over his heart, close his eyes for him, prop a rifle by his side—this is part of the job, part of creating a picture that will speak to the public. These pictures will show Americans what they are doing to themselves, and will help them decide if what they are doing is right. Your job is to fix the image for history.

PREPAR

OF TH

1.

THE PHOTOGRAPHER WHO
COULDN'T SEE
AND THE MAN FROM SCOTLAND

Well before the Civil War began, Mathew B. Brady was already a famous photographer and the proprietor of the most fashionable gallery in New York City. In the early 1840s he had studied the new art of making daguerreotypes with his mentor, Samuel F. B. Morse, and developed a highly successful business as a daguerreotype portraitist before turning to wet-plate photography. The Brady studio was a workshop of some twenty-five camera operators, artisans, painters, retouchers, framers, receptionists, and errand runners, and Brady presided over it as its impresario, the visionary artist at the center of a factory.[1] "In his hands a process, in itself mechanical, has become a plastic and graceful art, varied in its effects . . . and exerting a revolutionary influence upon general art, culture, and taste,"[2] wrote one magazine of Mathew Brady in 1858. Said another critic, "Mr. Brady resolved . . . to remove the prejudices which existed against [photography] by elevating

it into the dignity & beauty of an art of taste. . . . With the painter, everything depends upon the genius that guides the hand. In Photography, everything depends upon the skill with which the elements are prepared to make way for the hand of Nature."[3]

Brady was an effective salesman. He posed his sitters, controlled the lighting from skylights overhead, and arranged suitable props, all the while talking with the clients to put them at their ease. Unlike other studios, the Brady gallery had skylights that were tinted blue, which he claimed improved the image and gave a better quality of lighting to the face.[4] When he judged the composition to be just right, he signaled the camera operators to insert the sensitized glass plate into the camera and expose the negative. The actual operation of the camera and development of the negative were mere mechanical processes, quite separate from the work of the photographer, the artist. The

FIGURE 1

FIGURE 1
*Mathew B. Brady, self-
portrait. Date uncertain.
National Archives.*

FIGURE 2
*Portrait of Thomas Cole,
American landscape painter.
Mathew Brady. 1851.
Daguerreotype. National
Portrait Gallery.*

FIGURE 3
*Thaddeus Hyatt,
Abolitionist. Mathew Brady.
1857. Fogg Museum of Art,
Harvard University.*

B-1074

FIGURE 2

FIGURE 3

preparation of the composition was considered an art form itself, an act of theater for an appreciative audience that greeted the finished product with applause.[5] The atmosphere of art combined with science made the photography studio a sophisticated and high-toned establishment.[6]

Brady, who was charming and talkative, had a gift for staging the photograph, setting the subject at ease and drawing from the sitter his or her most characteristic expression. His portrait of esteemed landscape painter Thomas Cole shows the painter draped in the style of a Roman bust, a faraway look in his eyes, as if the artist has his gaze fixed on a distant classical landscape. This was the *art* of photography, and Brady had earned a significant reputation in this new field—a reputation as an artist.

Ironically, Brady's vision had been declining for years; even if he had chosen to operate the camera, he would have had difficulty doing so. But the role of the portrait photographer was to create the image that the camera would capture, and thus his failing eyesight was not a significant disability, and nobody found it odd that New York's most famous photographer saw so poorly, or that he protected his sensitive eyes with blue-tinted glasses.[7] "Mr. Brady is not operating [the camera] himself, a failing eyesight precluding the possibility of his using the camera with any certainty. But he is an excellent artist, nevertheless, understands his business perfectly, and gathers about him the finest talent to be found," reported *Photographic Art Journal* in 1851.[8] There was a clear distinction between the artist-photographer creating an image and the photographic operator who merely handled and processed the plate. Regardless of which assistant operated the camera at the Brady studio, the portraits were considered to be *by Brady.*

At some point in the 1840s Brady had hit upon the idea of creating a photographic catalogue of the most distinguished Americans, and had soon amassed an impressive collection, which was available for public view at his studio and gallery.[9] It was the first time photography had been put to work in the creation of a long-term historical record. The pursuit of his goal brought Brady into contact with politicians, artists, writers, performers, and dignitaries of all kinds, and he quickly became a master at the art of the celebrity portrait. No one could be considered a notable American without a place in the Brady gallery. His style of portraiture was simple and direct, beautifully lit, and uncomplicated by fussy props or allegorical costumes, as earlier portraits in aristocratic Europe had been. It was a style suited to the still-young republic of the United States.[10] The mid-1850s also saw the rise of the illustrated newspaper, such as *Frank Leslie's Illustrated Newspaper* and *Harper's Monthly,* and engravings based on Brady's portraits became a common feature in the media. "Photo by Brady" became synonymous with "portraits of important Americans."

In the same way as earlier American artists—portrait painters—had chosen columns and drapes as a way of referring back to classical Rome, Brady adopted these visual references to the earlier republic. He equipped his studio with columns and dark drapes and almost always used these in his portraits. It was part of his vision to help shape the national identity, even at a time when the nation itself was beginning to crack under pressure.

In 1851 Brady had been invited to display his work at the Great Exhibition in London, and had received a medal for his portraits. So great was the acclaim that Brady found himself with an international reputation and spent ten months traveling in Europe, meeting artists and aristocrats. It was during these months of travel that he made the acquaintance of Alexander Gardner, a Scotsman and fellow photographer-artist with a reputation of his own.[11]

Their meeting soon proved to be significant for both of them. Gardner, along with friends and family, had plans to emigrate to Iowa to form a Utopian settlement. In the spring of 1856 Gardner left Scotland to join the group, only to find the fledgling community already in a state of financial ruin. Disappointed, Gardner headed to New York City and contacted his colleague in the photographic arts, Mathew Brady.[12] In very short order Brady and Gardner had become partners in business.

It was a fruitful partnership. Brady, entertaining and charming, continued to work with the clientele of the gallery, but now Gardner turned his attention to the

FIGURE 4

practical matters of business. So successful was the team that in January of 1858, another Brady gallery opened in Washington, D.C., at 352 Pennsylvania Avenue—the better to continue adding photographic portraits of distinguished Americans to the Brady collection. Gardner left New York City to run the new gallery with his brother, James Gardner, and his apprentice, Timothy O'Sullivan.

The city of Washington was a quarrelsome place in 1858. Political tensions over slavery had been on the rise for years; the expansion of slavery into the territories was causing bitter division between North and South, and no solution other than *dissolution* of the Union lay on the horizon. Gardner and Brady, aware that Congress might soon lose its Southern senators and representatives, made a point of photographing politicians from both sides of the debate for the collection of distinguished Americans. It wouldn't be long before the only place senators and representatives from opposite sides of the abolition issue could be seen together was on the walls of a photographer's gallery.

TECHNIQUE

The process of wet plate photography involved several stages, some of them dangerous: First a sheet of glass (the plate) had to be evenly coated with a thin wet film of photographic collodion, a chemical solution containing cotton fibers. While still sticky the plate was sensitized in a darkroom with a bath of silver iodide, then placed in a lightproof holder. Before the plate dried, it had to be inserted into the camera and exposed. The operator removed the lens cap of the camera, exposing the wet plate to light coming through the lens. Exposure time depended on the amount of light available and varied from thirty seconds to over a minute (making action shots impossible). When the exposure was finished, the lens cap and lightproof case were replaced, and the plate was removed for developing and fixing in the darkroom.

The entire procedure, from filming the plate to developing and fixing the image, took approximately ten minutes. Once dried, the plate was varnished to protect the image from scratches. The result was a glass negative that could be used for printing multiple positive photographs. Photographic prints were direct prints, not enlargements, made the same size as the plate—so a large plate produced a large print, and a small plate produced a small print. To achieve a variety of sizes of photographs, the artist commonly used cameras of different sizes.

2.

THE MAN FROM ILLINOIS

On a blustery February day in 1860, Abraham Lincoln stopped in at Brady's New York gallery. The Illinois lawyer was scheduled to make a speech that night, his first major address to an eastern audience in his bid to win the Republican nomination for the presidential race. As a relative unknown outside his home state, Lincoln had his work cut out for him to develop a national reputation before the November election. Having his portrait made by the famous Mathew Brady was a surefire way to gain credibility.

The gallery was busy as usual that winter day. When Lincoln and his colleagues arrived, Brady welcomed them to the sky-lit studio, commonly called the "operating room,"[13] and immediately set about posing the tall—extremely tall—man from Illinois. A standing pose struck Brady as most suitable, but the immobilizer, the head brace used to keep the subject motionless during the exposure of the plate, was too short to reach Lincoln's head. It had to be set on a stool, carefully placed behind Lincoln to be out of view of the camera. Brady studied the effect, giving his customer an experienced appraisal. Maybe there was something about that long neck and protruding Adam's apple that struck Brady as a little too backwoods for a national political figure, a little too rough around the edges. Brady asked politely if he might rearrange Lincoln's collar, tugging it upward to hide some of that ungainly throat. Lincoln, never a man to miss making a joke at his own expense, laughed and agreed, and in that moment, even with the immobilizer clamped to the back of his head, he relaxed.[14]

The plate was exposed. Brady's operator hustled off to the darkroom to develop and fix the image. The photo session was over.

Later that night, with a snowstorm swirling through the dark streets of New York, Lincoln addressed the crowd at the Cooper Union hall. "Let us have faith that right makes might, and in that faith, let us, to the end, dare to do our duty as we understand it." His speech kept the audience captivated and was rewarded with heartfelt applause. In one night Lincoln became the man to watch.

FIGURE 5

Abraham Lincoln: the "Cooper Union portrait." Mathew Brady. February 27, 1860. Library of Congress.

And Brady had the photograph that showed the nation his face. The "Cooper Union portrait" was widely circulated to magazines and newspapers, where it was copied in engravings and printed for millions of Americans to see. What the public saw was a dignified, statesmanlike man, as tall and upright and dependable as a column. The Brady studio soon found that there was a huge public demand for the portrait and began printing card-size copies, which sold in the thousands.[15] In May Lincoln won the nomination of the Republican Party, and from then on this picture was everywhere.

The citizens of the Southern states did not look upon the face in this photograph with admiration. Far from it. Throughout his political career Lincoln had made legalistic arguments against the expansion of slavery. He was convinced that slavery was an institution whose day would end soon enough, and that there were constitutional reasons why newly formed territories and states could not permit slavery. He didn't argue the abolition of slavery in the states where it already existed, and during the presidential campaign he made repeated promises that he would not interfere with the slave states of the South.[16] But so emotional was the issue of abolition that neither side chose to see the careful distinction he was making. If Lincoln were elected, went the popular assumption, he would seek to abolish slavery. The slave states of the South were absolutely convinced of it—so convinced of it that South Carolina

made it perfectly clear that if Lincoln won in November, it would secede from the Union. The state would no longer be part of the United States.

In November Lincoln won the presidency.

On December 20, to the accompaniment of ringing church bells and artillery salvos, South Carolina voted to secede.[17]

A PHOTOGRAPH NOT TAKEN
This picture shows a modest kitchen. The lighting is poor—a vague midday light. Through the window indistinct tree shapes can be seen, but not clearly enough to make out what kind of tree, and therefore what kind of landscape—it could be Minnesota, it could be Alabama, or Vermont or Maryland or Florida. At the table the wife and husband are side-by-side, the newspaper full of bold headlines and subheads spread in front of them. But they are no longer looking at the newspaper: They are looking at the door, where their son, almost grown to manhood, has just walked in. The expressions on the couple's faces are quite different. The father wears a forced smile that is meant to convey pride but in fact masks envy of his son's youth, youth that can march and drill and carry a rifle musket. The mother's face is a mask of foreshadowed grief.

FIGURE 5

EXPO

SURE

3.

CARTE DE VISITE

Before the start of the new year, the point-of-no-return year of 1861, Alexander Gardner purchased some newfangled four-tube cameras for Brady's Washington gallery.[1] The four-tube camera could take four identical exposures on a single glass plate negative. The single plate could then be used to print four identical pictures at the same time, in this case *carte de visite* photos on cardboard—a popular format that allowed the sitter to give small (and inexpensive) photos to friends and loved ones. With war sounding an ominous drumbeat on the horizon and the certainty of young men being called to duty weighing heavily on everyone's heart, there was suddenly a huge demand for photographic mementoes. Brady himself was not a fan of the *carte de visite* format, which he felt cheapened photography and reduced the size of the portrait almost beyond all pretense of art.[2] But Gardner was the better businessman, and knew that the *carte de visite* business at a time like this was almost a license to print money—$1.00 for four prints.[3]

A steady run of secessions kept Brady's keepsake mills busy in both Washington and New York City. January 9: Mississippi. January 10: Florida. January 11: Alabama. January 19: Georgia. January 26: Louisiana. Rumors of war were now flying thick and fast, and the doors of the studios opened and shut, opened and shut on a chilly parade of *carte de visite* clients who took a number as they entered and waited their turns to be photographed.[4] Would Lincoln—who hadn't even been inaugurated yet, hadn't even left his home state of Illinois to head for the capital—put down this insurrection? Because it *was* an insurrection. It was a rebellion. There was no other way to describe what was happening. At home Lincoln was working on his inaugural speech and making preparations to move with his wife and young sons, Tad and Willie, to Washington. State militias from one end of the country to the other began drilling in courthouse squares and on town commons.

If Lincoln did order the rebellion put down, what would that mean, exactly? It was a historic test of the republic, no doubt about that. And historic events were now

FIGURE 6

FIGURE 6

a very uncertain future as president of a disintegrating republic. "I now leave, not knowing when, or whether ever, I may return, with a task before me greater than that which rested on Washington," he said upon leaving Springfield. Later that day, when the train huffed to a stop in Indianapolis, he told the crowd, "It is your business to rise up and preserve the Union and liberty, for yourselves, and not for me."[6]

Even as Lincoln made his way east, the commander of Fort Sumter, Major Robert Anderson, was in daily communication with Washington. Fort Sumter was a United States garrison guarding Charleston, South Carolina, from out in the bay—but the city that Anderson was sworn to protect had turned against him. South Carolina, the first to secede from the Union, was pre-

FIGURE 7

something that could be visually recorded as they happened. On January 31 Mathew Brady took out a loan of $3,628 against the contents of his New York City gallery[5]— whatever was about to happen, it had to be photographed, and Brady was already getting ready. Mortgaging his gallery must have seemed like a safe investment. Everyone would want photographs of whatever was coming.

February 1, Texas voted for secession. February 9, Jefferson Davis was elected provisional president of a new Confederate States of America. Two days later Lincoln departed his home, making his way toward

FIGURE 8

venting supplies from reaching the site, which it now considered an enemy fortification. Events were moving forward quickly, threatening to beat Lincoln to the capital.

He arrived on the twenty-third of the month in a city boiling with anticipation. On Capitol Hill the dome of the great capitol stood awkward and exposed, showing its innards to the wintry sky like an opened egg: Plans for a renovation of the building had gone forward, a strange irony considering that the country it represented was about to undergo a savage renovation of its own. Below the cracked egg of the dome the building echoed with the urgent whispers and exclamations of the fragmented Congress. The unfinished Washington Monu-ment, only one third its intended size, stood like a dead tree stump.[7] To a stranger it must have been hard to tell if the city was half built or half destroyed.

The soon-to-be president made the Brady studio one of his very first stops, intending to get his first presidential portrait over with. Lincoln, with the collapsing Union commanding his thoughts, "seemed absolutely indifferent to all that was going on about him," said a young artist who assisted Brady and Gardner that day. "And he gave the impression that he was a man overwhelmed with anxiety and fatigue and care."[8]

Overwhelmed as he was, the president-elect sat in a dark cloud of solitude as

FIGURE 9

9th N.Y. Volunteer Infantry.
Mathew Brady Studio. CA.
1861. National Archives.
    Note the skylight in the
upper right corner of the
frame; this picture would
normally have been cropped
to delete that part of the
studio technology.

FIGURE 9

Gardner took five exposures, and only made an effort to be sociable when he reintroduced himself to Mathew Brady. "Brady and the Cooper Union Speech made me president," he said, shaking the famous photographer's hand.[9] No doubt Brady was flattered by the compliment.

The inauguration was on March 4. At one in the afternoon a crowd of some 30,000 gathered on the lawn of the Capitol, keeping out of puddles and skirting construction equipment and artillery. Uniformed soldiers lined the streets, and marksmen watched for snipers. There was no denying that Washington was actually a southern city: Virginia lay just across the Potomac, and at its back was Maryland, another slave state, although one that so far showed no signs of rebellion. The capital of the republic lay on the front porch of the insurrection, and it was safe to assume that not everyone in the milling crowd was a supporter of Abraham Lincoln. So the troops were there in force, as well as undercover detectives. It was partly cloudy, with temperatures in the fifties. As Lincoln rose to deliver his address, he discovered that there was no place for him to put his hat. A senator nearby reached to take it.

"In your hands, my dissatisfied fellow countrymen, and not in mine, is the momentous issue of civil war," Lincoln warned. "The government will not assail you. You can have no conflict without being yourselves the aggressors."[10]

Meanwhile, urgent news from Fort Sumter arrived on the same day. Supplies were about to run out, and it would take 20,000 Federal troops to reinforce the garrison effectively against South Carolina's hostility. Something had to be done, and quickly. "Assuming it to be possible to now provision Fort Sumter, under all circumstances, is it wise to attempt it?"[11] the new president asked his cabinet. It was clear that if they did provision and reinforce the fort, it would probably be the match that lit the fuse.

State volunteer militias began forming in earnest, readying themselves for a war that many were eager for. Young men resplendent in new uniforms stood proudly in front of cameras from north to south, harboring secret fears: fears that the fray would be over before they could take part; fears that if they did take part, they might not do credit to their states and their country. The *carte de visite* mills continued to grind.

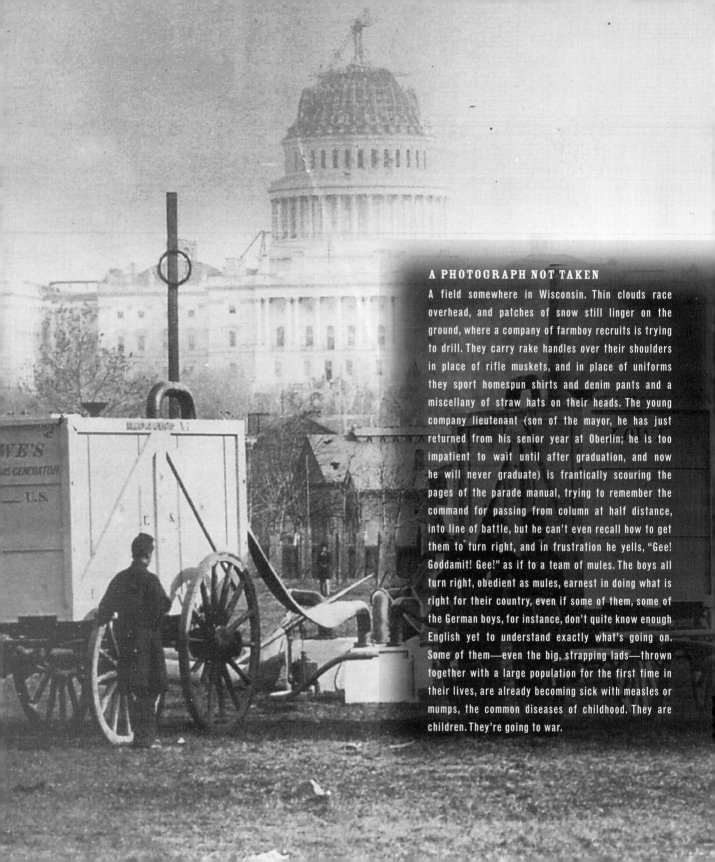

A PHOTOGRAPH NOT TAKEN

A field somewhere in Wisconsin. Thin clouds race overhead, and patches of snow still linger on the ground, where a company of farmboy recruits is trying to drill. They carry rake handles over their shoulders in place of rifle muskets, and in place of uniforms they sport homespun shirts and denim pants and a miscellany of straw hats on their heads. The young company lieutenant (son of the mayor, he has just returned from his senior year at Oberlin; he is too impatient to wait until after graduation, and now he will never graduate) is frantically scouring the pages of the parade manual, trying to remember the command for passing from column at half distance, into line of battle, but he can't even recall how to get them to turn right, and in frustration he yells, "Gee! Goddamit! Gee!" as if to a team of mules. The boys all turn right, obedient as mules, earnest in doing what is right for their country, even if some of them, some of the German boys, for instance, don't quite know enough English yet to understand exactly what's going on. Some of them—even the big, strapping lads—thrown together with a large population for the first time in their lives, are already becoming sick with measles or mumps, the common diseases of childhood. They are children. They're going to war.

4.

FIRST SHOTS

It didn't take long for the tension to reach the breaking point. Throughout Lincoln's first month in office, telegrams and communiqués went back and forth between Washington and Fort Sumter. War rumors and speculation were on everyone's lips. In early April, Lincoln informed the governor of South Carolina that resupply ships were on their way to Fort Sumter, and that any interference with Federal troops would be considered an act of war. South Carolina's response was a blunt demand for the surrender of the fort, and on April 12 the state began firing from batteries on the Charleston waterfront.

The outbreak of war "brings a feeling of relief: the suspense is over," remarked an Ohio senator.[12] On April 13, U.S. flags were taken down throughout the South and state flags run up in their place,[13] while in the North loyal Union women trimmed their bonnets with red, white, and blue ribbons, and bands from little towns to major cities played *The Star-Spangled Banner* in the streets; horses hitched to omnibuses in Union cities were decorated with bunting and flags.[14]

At Fort Sumter, Major Anderson and his small force were being pummeled, and they had no choice but to surrender.

When the news reached the president, Lincoln immediately called for 75,000 state volunteer troops to help put down the rebellion. Three days layer Virginia voted to join the Confederacy. Now that war was imminent, it was time for everyone to declare sides. Southern employees of the federal government packed up their bags and left Washington for their home states; officers of the army and navy whose home states had seceded resigned their commissions.

Lincoln awaited his troops, knowing full well that he faced a rebellious Virginia on one side and an undeclared Maryland on the other. Would Maryland allow Federal troops to travel through to the capital? He could actually see, across the Potomac, Confederate troops camped at Arlington.[15] On April 23 he stood at the window of the White House, looking anxiously toward the Potomac, and muttered, "Why don't they come? Why don't they come?"[16] Two days later they came. The 7th New York marched down Pennsylvania Avenue to the cheers of thousands of Union loyalists who lined the street, waving flags. Lincoln watched, holding his sons Tad and Willie by the hand.[17]

With the opening of the war and the call for troops, the photography galleries were inundated with fresh waves of soldiers posing for photos. Regiments arrived in Washington every week and began setting up encampments all over the city. The White House itself was overrun with soldiers stopping by for a look-see, since it was every citizen's right to enter the building and even ask to meet the president.[18] In early May, Confederate troops abandoned Alexandria, and Federal troops crossed the Potomac and moved in by the end of the month. Richmond, Virginia, became the new Confederate capital, a move that marked Richmond—and much of Virginia—for destruction and devastation.

Preparations continued at a feverish pace, with volunteer regiments pouring into Washington. Numerous small skirmishes were beginning to blaze up in Virginia and in some of the western states along the Mississippi. At the end of June a brilliant comet streaked across the night sky like an artillery fuse. Spiritualist mediums were all the rage in Washington,[19] and the comet must have figured in many a séance's predictions; citizens were already thinking about how to communicate with the dear departed.

The summer fighting season was ready to open.

FIGURE 10

5.

OPERATORS IN THE FIELD

Whose idea was it to photograph the war? Afterward both Brady and Gardner claimed credit for the original inspiration. It was certainly right up Brady's alley, using photographs to document history. And he had already supplied himself with a fistful of cash to pay for equipment. He was also the one with the best connections, and he used them well, applying first to the influential General Winfield Scott and to Brigadier General Irvin McDowell, the newly appointed commander of the Department of Northeastern Virginia (the Union army),[20] who told him to ask at the White House. Allan Pinkerton, head of the Secret Service, made no objection to Brady photographing the war but couldn't offer any protection. Brady even went to the president, who casually scrawled "Pass Brady. A. Lincoln" on a sheet of paper for his celebrity photographer.[21] Then "I finally secured permission from Edwin Stanton, the Secretary of War, to go onto the battlefields with my cameras," Brady later said.[22]

Whoever thought of it first, it was a monumental task that required financing and planning. Gardner struck a deal with photographic suppliers E. & H. T. Anthony to reproduce wartime images on a massive scale for sale to the public, while paying the Brady Gallery a percentage of the profits and crediting each image as a "Photo by Brady."[23]

And Brady went to work hiring and outfitting a small army of photographic operators, the men who would actually be out in the theater of war taking the pictures. Each team would be equipped with a What-Is-It Wagon, a darkroom on wheels that would carry the cameras, chemicals, and glass plates needed to capture the scenes of camp life and battleground. It was an "ordinary wagon . . . [with a] strong step attached at the rear and below the level of the wagon floor," explained one photographer. "A door was put on at back, carefully hung so as to be lightproof."[24] The operators' assignment would be to expose and develop plates in the field, and return periodically to the gallery to have the photographs printed.

Exactly what the operators were supposed to do, what specific orders they had

from Brady, or what subjects they were asked to shoot, is unrecorded. They were severely limited in what and when and where they could photograph, for several reasons. They were at the mercy of the weather and the sunlight, of course. Because they could use only natural lighting, photographs were generally made in the brightest hours of the day, between ten and two. But even in the strongest sunlight, which reduced exposure time to as little as five to ten seconds, any motion in the scene would create a blur on the negative.[25] As a result, all photographs either were posed portraits or were of stationary objects or scenery. There were no action shots.

Another technical limitation was the need for clean water. The entire process of preparing, exposing, and developing a wet collodion negative took ten minutes and relied on a supply of clean, clear water for much of the processing. Photographers on the march with the army seldom had the luxury of an uncontaminated water source.

Yet another curb on the operators' chances was the quasi-official status of the photographers. Some of the operators had more or less ambiguous relationships with the army,[26] and some simply roved where they could. Even at the best of times they were consigned to the rear, at the dusty end of a marching column, behind the train of baggage and ammunition wagons—hours behind the front end. When photographers were in the vicinity of the battle action, they were prevented from going forward until the fighting was over. There was simply no place for a photographer and his delicate, bulky equipment amid the clangor and frenzy of battle.

As a result, most of the photographs of the war are deceptively placid. A great many of them show soldiers in camp, where the operators tried to mimic the conventions of the studio, substituting a tree

FIGURE 12

even easier were dead soldiers, who didn't need to be told to keep perfectly still. In July of 1861, however, the subjects of those photographs were still living, breathing soldiers.

FIGURE 11

trunk for a classical column, tent flaps for dramatic draperies.[27] Even photographs of ruined landscapes were placid, because they depicted stillness, the absence of action and life.

It would be stillness, and the absence of life, that created the most memorable of the photographs. Living soldiers standing motionless made for easy subjects—but

A PHOTOGRAPH NOT TAKEN

July 4, 1861: Nighttime, the comet still visible, and now in this instant joined by fireworks exploding over the capital. Two small, tired girls in matching straw hats decorated with blue ribbons stand with their arms around each other's waists. Their upturned faces are flanked by the small flags each holds by their sticks. They've been allowed to stay up long past their usual bedtime; they watched the great military review down Pennsylvania Avenue earlier in the day, complete with bands and drummer boys and "Yankee Doodle Dandy," and cannon and rifle salutes, and the thrilling ranks of dancing, dashing cavalry horses nodding their heads. There are over 58,000 volunteer soldiers in and around Washington and it seemed as though every single one of them marched in the parade today, to the cries of "Forward to Richmond!" from the spectators. Now, as an especially loud firework bursts overhead, both girls flinch and begin to cry. It's been a long day, and the chatter of firecrackers is no longer exciting. They're frightened. They want to go home.

6.

"YANKEE DOODLE DANDY"

In mid-July the Union army began a movement into Virginia, toward Confederate forces near the town of Manassas, Virginia. They sang "John Brown's Body" as they marched, and joked that Manassas was just a quick stop on the way to Richmond. Billy Yank was going to whip Johnny Reb and be back in Washington for some dancing and light refreshments.

As the Confederate troops fell back, away from the Union advance, Brady took a notion to supervise the first major battle photographs of his great plan[28] and packed up a What-Is-It Wagon and an assistant and some friends and headed after the army. It was clear to military and civilian personnel alike that the troops would clash at Manassas, and so the railroad junction near the little creek called Bull Run became the destination for hundreds of war-hungry citizens. "Every carriage, gig, wagon, and hack has been engaged by people going out to see the fight. . . . [T]he hotel-keepers . . . must treble the prices of their wines and of the hampers of provisions that the Washington people are ordering to comfort themselves

at their bloody Derby,"[29] wrote a London newspaper reporter on the scene. It was a lovely summer Sunday, and folks thought it was a grand idea to take a picnic out to watch the fighting—and then be able to say they'd witnessed the Civil War. Few people in the Union thought the rebel forces could put up much of a fight against the mighty war machine of the United States army. The insurrection would be quashed, and then it would all be over. The march to Manassas was like the Independence Day parade all over again.

But when the battle got underway, fortune took a surprising turn: Resistance from the Confederate troops was fiercer than expected, and the Federal commanders tried to call for a retreat. But the volunteer army had been training for only a few months, and few officers and regiments knew how to manage an orderly retreat. To make things worse, progress back toward Washington was strangled by narrow bridges over the creeks and streams, and the traffic jam of carriages full of spectators soon created an utter snarl. Panic, miscommunication,

FIGURE 13
*Bull Run, Va. View of the
battlefield. Photographer
unknown. 1861. Library of
Congress.*

civilians bumbling through the troops, horse-drawn artillery, overturned wagons, oncoming ambulances—the worse it got, the more panicked people became. "The road was filled with wagons, artillery, retreating cavalry and infantry in one confused mass," wrote an observer, "each seemingly bent on looking out for number one and letting the rest do the same."[30]

In the turmoil Brady's wagon was overturned, smashing all the plates and apparatus he'd brought along and pitching him into the muddle of people retreating on foot. He fell in with a company made up of firemen from New York City, who offered him a long sword to protect himself with.[31] The next day, footsore and covered with dust and grime, he made it back to Washington with not a single picture to show for the effort. The first major battle of the war went unphotographed.

He did, however, make his own studio his first stop, and he had himself photographed in his "battle uniform." It was to be the start of a pattern for Brady, who made sure that not only his name but his image would become part of the photographic documentation. The bearded, bespectacled New Yorker in the dandy straw boater would soon be as familiar to Americans as Lincoln himself.

After the Battle of Bull Run (later called the *First* Battle of Bull Run, after the site became a battlefield again a year later), the war took on a different tone in the United States. It was odd, it was perplexing: The

GEN'L. GEO. B. McCLELLAN.

Entered according to Act of Congress in the year 1861, by M B. Brady, in the Clerks' office of the District Court of the District of Columbia.

Federal troops *should* have beaten the Rebels, and yet it hadn't happened that way. Far from it. The boom of artillery from the fighting had been audible in Washington, a mere thirty miles away,[32] and now it didn't seem so much like an occasion for picnics and carriage rides. The Confederates were celebrating a resounding victory, and the United States military in general—and General Irvin McDowell in particular— was looking inept.

It was time for a new general.

Out in the western theater of the war a young, handsome (and not particularly tall) West Pointer named George Brinton McClellan had had several victories early in the summer. With the wounded from Bull Run still lying on stretchers, McDowell was relieved of command of the army and McClellan put in his place, at the head of what was now called the Division of the Potomac. Before long he was known to an optimistic Union as Little Mac. Newspapers hailed him as the Young Napoleon.[33]

If lack of military training and discipline had been partly to blame for the fiasco at Bull Run, Little Mac vowed to whip the troops into shape and make them feel like an army. What the army—and the country—needed was a great show of

FIGURE 15

taken
ly.22d
1861

BRADY
The Photographer
returned from

martial splendor to rekindle their enthusiasm for war. Almost his very first order of business when he assumed command in August was to schedule a grand review of the troops, with eight regiments of infantry, along with artillery and cavalry formations, "the finest sight I believe I ever seen,"[34] wrote a soldier. The soldiers cheered as President Lincoln rode past in an open carriage. McClellan seemed to think military reviews were the chief purpose of commanding the army: He scheduled them often, and when the men were lined up in their ranks and the officers stood with swords drawn, he would gallop down the field on a big black horse, his escort galloping behind as the bands played and artillery batteries fired salutes. It was a grand, impressive sight for the senators and other bigwigs who watched from their carriages. McClellan's bravado seemed to make people feel that things were getting done, and his popularity increased as the year continued. It wouldn't be long before he was offered command of the whole army, both east and west, a big job for a young officer, but "I can do it all," he boasted.[35]

But while the jaunty McClellan drilled and paraded the army around Washington, the war ground to a halt.

7.

ALL QUIET ALONG THE POTOMAC

"How long would it require to actually get in motion?" Lincoln wrote to McClellan in early December.[36]

Of all the Union loyalists in Washington, Lincoln seemed to be the only one not entirely *overwhelmed* with General McClellan. He made frequent visits to the training camps outside the city, asking when the army would go fight the rebels. McClellan found the president's inquiries an irritation and kept Lincoln waiting, sometimes even ignoring him completely. But the president was dogged and refused to make a personal issue out of something—the war—that was so critical to the nation's future. "I will hold McClellan's horse if he will only bring us success," he remarked with his usual dryness.[37]

But in the fall the troops hadn't been ready, and winter was not the time for fighting—and there was always a good reason for not getting started. McClellan's officers spent much of their time in the city, dining at hotels and enjoying Washington hospitality, while the soldiers were required to stay in camp.[38] Discipline was loose or nonexistent, and men entertained themselves with drinking and brawling. There wasn't much else to do, other than get sick from the poor sanitation[39] or examine their bodies for lice. Occasionally a wave of religious revivalism would break over the camp; it was something to do, anyway.[40]

There wasn't much to photograph, either, and the image makers had to do their best with scenes of camp life or marching drills. Brady continued to recruit and train field operators, making ready for the spring fighting weather.[41] With assistance from the head of the Secret Service, Alexander Gardner managed to get an appointment to McClellan's staff in the Topographical Engineers to photograph maps and charts, even though he was still formally employed by the Brady Gallery.[42] It gave him free access to the camps, along with opportunities to take photographs of soldiers to send back to the studio. What the photos showed, and what the newspapers reported, was "All Quiet Along the Potomac."

Small actions were ongoing around Virginia, where already winter campfires

FIGURE 16
Ambulance Crew Drill,
Unknown Location.
Unknown Photographer.
Unknown Date. Library of
Congress.
    The troops are dressed as
Zouaves; this was one of the
colorful styles of uniform
many regiments selected for
themselves early in the war.
It wasn't until later that
uniforms became uniform.

had stripped surrounding farmhouses of their clapboards and roofs. Soldiers on picket duty in Virginia that December stood around fires made of fence rails.[43] The fencing style in those parts didn't require posts. They were just "lazy" fences, the rails stacked at zigzag angles, and with the rails burned for firewood, it was as if there were no boundaries, no borders, no reason to fight.

Snow fell. In the capital 150 horses died in a fire at a government stable on Christmas. Wagon wheels churned mud and snow in the Union army camps to mule-bogging goo, and it was obvious there would be no movement of troops. "As a defense to the enemy this Virginia mud is as good as several regiments to their numbers, as it prevents us from raiding or attacking them, for neither army can march two miles in the filthy red pasty mud," wrote a soldier.[44] Everyone was stuck.

Local peddlers and vendors set up cook shops near the camps. As a supplement to the army diet soldiers could get eggs cooked to order, pancakes, apple fritters[45]—almost anything, as long as they could pay for it. A private's pay was thirteen dollars a month.[46] Aside from endless drilling and marching, marching and drilling, camp life didn't offer much in the way of entertainment; buying special treats from the vendors was a welcome distraction—sixty cents a pound for butter, fifty cents a pound for cheese, whiskey at a dollar a shot.[47] The young men who had enlisted so eagerly were discovering the reality of army life: When they rested, they had more rest than they needed, but when it came time to act, they would have far more action than they wanted. As soldier Oliver Wendell Holmes, Jr. (later to become a Supreme Court Judge) observed, "War is an organized bore."[48]

With mounting frustration President Lincoln issued Proclamation General War Order #1 at the end of January. "Ordered that the 22nd of February 1862 be the day for a general movement of the Land and Naval forces of the United States against the insurgent forces."[49]

So it was down in the law books now. McClellan would have to set his enormous Division of the Potomac into motion by Washington's Birthday. Early in February the King of Siam offered President Lincoln some war elephants, although the president declined the tropical assistance as politely as he could. The United States "does not reach a latitude so low as to favor the multiplication of the elephant,"[50] he explained in his letter turning down the gift. Artillery crews practiced firing, learning to spring out of the way as the limbers—carts to which gun carriages were attached—jumped backward, gouging deep gashes in the cold mud. The snow continued falling.

And then there was finally some cause for celebration; from across the mountains, news arrived that Fort Donelson on the Mississippi had fallen to a tough western general named Ulysses S. Grant, who had demanded "unconditional surrender" of the rebel forces there. U. S. Grant: People began to say the U.S. stood for "unconditional surrender" and turned a skeptical eye toward McClellan. Washington's Birthday was just days away. It was time for something to happen.

8.

TO THE GATES OF RICHMOND— OR HALFWAY, ANYWAY

"My boy is gone. He is actually gone."[51] The Lincoln family was rocked by twelve-year-old Willie's death from typhoid fever. Mrs. Lincoln was inconsolable, and the president wept in his office, reading the casualty lists from Grant's victory at Fort Donelson. For each soldier killed there was a mother or father at home who felt the same bottomless grief he felt now. His little son Tad was with him, just a little boy, but his son Robert—Robert was as old as many of the recruits—it didn't bear thinking of. And the deadline for sending more soldiers into action was only two days away.

Washington's Birthday arrived, the day for deploying McClellan's troops. With the rising sun cannon salutes were fired in the Navy Yard and surrounding forts of the capital, rattling the windows in the city and rousing the citizens from their beds. The army began its slow progress out of the city. Hundreds of cattle lowed and groaned as they were driven across Long Bridge, and Pennsylvania Avenue was clogged by long wagon trains.[52] At long last, movement.

The enemy capital of Richmond, Virginia, lay about a hundred miles from Washington. But as March got underway, it was clear that Little Mac's plan was anything but direct. Rather than head due south for the rebel capital, he would go by water down Chesapeake Bay, and up the James River, rounding the Virginia Peninsula and coming at Richmond from below. The army began to assemble itself at Alexandria, Annapolis, and Washington, while in the rivers prowling gunboats began the work of clearing rebel batteries.* By March 17 the way was open for the embarkation of 100,000 Federal troops.

The embarkation of the army was a mammoth project. Hundreds of boats of all kinds were pressed into service. Lincoln himself boarded a government boat and whittled for hours as the first vessels began to head down the Potomac[53] for Fort Monroe in Hampton, Virginia. Braying mules and artillery horses were hoisted onto barges by sling, while out on the river regiments called back and forth across the

*ON MARCH 9, 1862, THE HISTORIC CLASH BETWEEN THE FIRST TWO "MODERN" NAVAL BATTLESHIPS, THE U.S.S. *MONITOR* AND THE C.S.S. *MERRIMAC,* TOOK PLACE OFF THE MOUTH OF THE JAMES RIVER. IT ENDED IN A DRAW WITH BOTH SHIPS DAMAGED; BUT THE ADVANTAGE WENT TO THE FEDERAL FORCES, BECAUSE THE *MERRIMAC* WAS OUT OF COMMISSION AND COULD NOT PROTECT VIRGINIA FROM TROOPS AS THEY MOVED DOWN TO THE VIRGINIA PENINSULA.

FIGURE 18

FIGURE 17

Fugitive slaves fording the Rappahannock River. Timothy O'Sullivan (Brady Studio). Library of Congress.

On June 19 Lincoln signed a law prohibiting slavery in U.S. territories, and on July 17 the Confiscation Act, making all slaves free once they came under the protection of the Union army; the Emancipation Proclamation was still months away.

FIGURE 18

Landing supplies on the James River. Brady Studio. Date unknown. National Archives.

FIGURE 19

Cumberland Landing, Va.: Group of "contrabands" (runaway slaves) at Foller's House. James Gibson. May 14, 1862. Library of Congress.

water to other regiments.[54] Flags snapped in the spring breeze. On almost every troop transport, regimental bands filled the air with patriotic tunes; men, women, and children on civilian craft cheered as the soldiers steamed by.[55] A shortage of coal kept some steamships delayed at the docks,[56] but on the whole the embarkation went forward. The river saw an endless parade of boats through the last weeks of March. By the end of the month 121,500 men, 14,592 animals, 1,224 wagons and ambulances, and 44 artillery batteries had been transported to Fort Monroe.[57]

At Fort Monroe, out on the tip of the Virginia Peninsula, two wharves were available for the steamers. As fast as one ship was

FIGURE 17

off-loaded, it was shuttled aside to make room for another.[58] Hundreds of soldiers stacked their muskets along a mile of beach, while the officers stormed the Hygeia Hotel for ale and fresh oysters at fifty cents a dozen.[59] There was a drizzling snow mixed with rain on March 23, but signs of spring were everywhere nonetheless: Azaleas were beginning to bloom, and daffodils swayed in the breeze.[60] The Army of the Potomac began to move up the peninsula at the rate of one division per day.[61] Troops moved overland, leaving the sodden roads for the use of the wagon trains.[62]

Along with the steady progress of baggage, supply, and ammunition wagons, there were What-Is-It Wagons. Brady operators exposed plates when they could, moved when they had to, urging their mules through the muck and mire at the backs of the endless six-mule-team wagon trains. Thanks to frequent spring rainstorms, wagons sometimes bogged up to their axles in mud, and mules

frequently wallowed in it to rid themselves of their harnesses and be free of their killing burdens. Everyone was covered head to toe in mud, and the odds of finding clean water for washing photographic plates were slim. Heavy thunderstorms brought more than mud—lightning sometimes killed men where they stood, and maddened the mules,

a Union soldier to his family, "it was with the burning embers taken from the ruins of what a few hours before had been a happy home."[66] Clapboards were stripped from houses, fences were dismantled, and trees were felled to feed the army's cook fires, and the countryside was soon a desolate landscape. Slaves who had liberated themselves from their absconding owners followed the Union soldiers, seeking protection. It was an entire peninsula on the move, even the mud getting up and rushing away, clinging to the hooves of cattle as they stampeded from the commissaries near the brigade camps.

FIGURE 19

Foraging was discouraged, and soldiers were told they must not help themselves to sheep or pigs, but as one soldier said, "[O]ccasionally we captured a big rabbit— sometimes with wool and sometimes with bristles."[67] Acts of "treason" by rebel livestock (a goose hissing at a Union flag, a bull lowering its head as if to charge a column of soldiers) were punished by the offending animal's becoming dinner.[68] What might appear remarkably like a farmer's fat hog roasting over a soldier's cookfire was explained with a wink as "slow deer." Occasionally a gang of quail or wild turkey

horses, and commissary cattle herds.[63] By April 4 it was warm enough to swim in the James River,[64] and frogs croaked in the swamps at night in counterpoint to the braying of mules.[65]

The Virginians who lived in the area scattered in advance of the United States troops, abandoning their farms. "Each time we lighted our pipes that day," wrote

FIGURE 20

FIGURE 21

wave of U.S. soldiers crept forward as timidly as a troop of orphans. Rain continued to fall, and artillery fire answered the thunder while the Federals dug in siege positions. Members of the signal corps climbed trees to get a view of what was happening beyond the fortifications, and when a tree they were in was hit by artillery, they climbed another.[70]

The Confederate troops evacuated Yorktown in early May, and when McClellan led his troops into the city the next day, he bragged, "The success is brilliant." But by the end of May the army was still tiptoeing up the peninsula, still far from its objective. "I think the time is near when you must either attack Richmond or give up the job and come to the defense of Washington,"[71] Lincoln told the general.

ran through camp—or halfway, anyway.[69]

With the advance of the huge Union force up the peninsula, there were frequent skirmishes and firefights, but the Confederate forces fell back against the overpowering strength of McClellan's army. Holing up at Yorktown, a rebel force of only 15,000 held off the Federals; McClellan, cautious despite his huge advantage, held back, giving the Confederates time to reinforce their position. What should have been a tidal

McClellan would have none of it. Battles were now more frequent and violent; and the redbud trees were in bloom, giving the landscape a blood-spattered effect. McClellan split his forces and sent three corps northeast of the Chickahominy River, expecting to meet additional Federal troops moving in from the north. But the terrain around the Chickahominy was marshy and flooded by the constant rains, and the troops continued to be bogged down by mud and swamps and sickened with malaria and diseases brought on by dirty water. Heat prostrated men who dropped in their tracks on long marches; mosquitoes grew fat. Confederate General Robert E. Lee knew that Richmond could not withstand a siege, so when another sudden rainstorm flooded the Chickahominy, dividing McClellan's forces, the Confederate army seized the advantage and attacked,[72] with punishing effect. The round musket balls the rebel troops used were strangely quiet as they cut through the air, and often the only sound they made was the popping of leaves as the bullets ripped through.[73] The Peninsula Campaign was turning out to be a costly mistake. Richmond would not be seized; McClellan took his big army and retreated, the men cutting ripe wheat from fields at the sides of the road to fill their haversacks as they went.[74]

The photographers did what they could, given the constant movement and the almost ceaseless rain that kept the lawns of the James River plantations deeply green and the streams churned with mud. James Gibson, a Brady operator, followed close behind the action of the Seven Days' Battles and recorded wounded Union soldiers sprawled on the ground outside a field hospital, seeking relief from the scorching heat. The grass beneath them was saturated with blood, and a stench worse than a slaughterhouse drew swarms of flies.[75] The tormented soldiers he caught in his photograph, members of the 16th New York Infantry, were too ill or disabled to be moved, and were abandoned when the army began evacuating.

FIGURE 22

FIGURE 23

Wounded Federal soldiers in a field hospital at Savage Station. James Gibson. June 28, 1862. Library of Congress.

The soldiers here had been wounded at the battles of Oak Grove, Gaines' Mill, and Mechanicsville, in the Seven Days' Battles, and were abandoned when the Union army evacuated to Harrison's Landing on the James River. Tons of Union stores were abandoned along with the soldiers, and were destroyed rather than allowed to fall into the hands of the enemy. Flour, bales of hay, crates of hardtack, clothing, arms, and reserve ammunition went up in flames.

FIGURE 24

FIGURE 24
*Military bridge built by
15ᵗʰ N.Y. Volunteers. James
Gibson (Brady Studio).
Library of Congress.*

They were taken prisoner two days later. By the time the public saw the photo, it was a photograph of ghosts.

Brady's operators, at Gardner's direction, were also taking photographs wherever and whenever possible for the Corps of Engineers—taking views of railroad bridges, roads, signal tower positions. Anything that could help the field commanders take the lay of the land prior to battle was useful,[76] and many of these photographs ended up as engravings in the illustrated newspapers or on public display at the galleries. Americans for the first time could see the land of battle: The towns and rivers named in their sons' and brothers' letters were no longer distant and unimaginable places. "All who follow the army with their private hearts as well as their public hopes will see with curious satisfaction the roads, the fields, the woods, the fences, the bridges, the camps, and the streams which are the familiar daily objects

FIGURE 24

to the eyes of their loved soldier boys," wrote the editors of *Harper's Weekly*.[77]

And it was Mathew Brady who had earned the credit for making this possible. "Brady's Photographic Corps" had become as common on the battlefield as the telegraph operators and the balloonists. "The public is indebted to Brady of Broadway for numerous excellent views of 'grim-visaged war,'"[78] the papers were saying. By the time the ill-fated and expensive Peninsula Campaign was over, "Photo by Brady" was firmly stamped on the public's perception of the war.

9.

EXPOSED

Bad news from the peninsula did little to diminish the July 4 celebrations in the North, but the campaign had been a costly failure: Richmond remained unchallenged, and Little Mac's star had lost its shine. With the Federal troops resting and resupplying at Harrison's Landing, a plantation on the James River, Lincoln boarded the steamer *Ariel* on July 8 to visit his soldiers. The boat ran aground on a sandbar, and the president took the opportunity to go swimming while he waited for the *Ariel* to be winched free.[79] He finally arrived late that night and reviewed the troops by moonlight. The Army of the Potomac was sick, hot, wet, wounded, and weary. Evacuation began as soon as possible, and would take another month to complete. Week by week the wounded arrived in the capital, which had become one enormous hospital. A steady parade of ambulances ferried the wounded from the steamer landings on the Potomac to hospitals throughout the city. Mortuary tents added the reek of embalming to the humid summer air.

Now was not the time for Lincoln to make his most important proposal. But on July 22, he presented the cabinet with his Emancipation Proclamation. Secretary of State William Seward recommended that the president delay. The Union was desperate for a victory, some evidence that they were on the right course. *Wait. Wait. The public will not support this unholy slaughter if it becomes a war to free the slaves.*

Lincoln *was* desperate for victory. With so many more men, so many more factories and armories and ships and ports and railroads at his disposal, he still could not put down the rebellion. As if to reinforce his continuing failure, reports of the Second Battle of Bull Run—a repeat of the first Union defeat—arrived on Lincoln's desk in late August.

By this time Brady had men in thirty-five bases in all theaters of the war,[80] and the newspapers were well supplied with photographs to make engravings from. The illustrated press kept the public—and the soldiers themselves—very well informed on the activities of the army. How could this General Lee enjoy nothing but victory?

FIGURE 25

Field headquarters of the New York Herald *newspaper. Timothy O'Sullivan. August 1863. Library of Congress.*

Major northern newspapers had war correspondents with the army to gather news, and also newspaper vendors to keep the troops informed. Harper's Weekly *and* Atlantic *were popular magazines in camp, and the New York papers were available in camp two days old for 10¢.*

FIGURE 26

Gen. George B. McClellan and staff. Brady Studio. National Archives.

FIGURE 27

Virginia. Newspaper vendor and cart in camp. Alexander Gardner. Library of Congress.

FIGURE 25

asked citizens on street corners. How could he move without effective resistance so close to Washington? Was the capital safe, exposed as it was to this deadly general? Was it possible this war was completely misguided? What was this war for? Why was it necessary for so many to die?

FIGURE 26

FIGURE 27

DEVELOP

TH

10.

THE BLOODIEST DAY

General Lee. *General Lee.* Confound the man! How was he managing to do it? He knew attacking Washington directly was futile—by now the city was ringed with fortifications, and the entire Army of the Potomac was encamped within the city limits or close outside. Lee's home state of Virginia was pummeled and battered after so much military campaigning, and as September opened its golden arms, General Lee carried the war out of Virginia and into the Union itself: He invaded Maryland—one of the only slave states to remain loyal to the United States.

While government department clerks played baseball on the grounds of the White House, the Army of the Potomac hustled itself to chase Lee; regiments began marching out of Washington, passing alongside the carriages of the wealthy on leafy suburban streets. The Peninsula Campaign veterans had lived on army rations for so long (some of them ill with scurvy) that they could not resist helping themselves to the ripe fruit of the Maryland countryside: peaches, pears, and apples.[1] Women came to their front porches and waved their handkerchiefs as McClellan's troops tramped by. For the first time, Union forces were moving through a pro-Union countryside, and in spite of lice and hard marching, morale began to climb. "I almost forgot the war and the fact that I was a soldier as I gained the summit of the first range of mountains, and the Cumberland Valley was spread out before me," a Pennsylvania soldier recalled of the march into Maryland.[2]

If moving into Maryland was good for Federal morale, it had the opposite effect on southern troops. Men began to melt away from the Army of Northern Virginia as it crossed into Northern territory: What they had seen as an invasion of the South was apparently finished, and the many poor and shoeless soldiers of Lee's ill-equipped army found the hard Maryland roads too punishing to their bare feet.[3]

The town of Frederick was occupied for nearly a week by Lee's forces; when the Army of the Potomac arrived on September 13, the dwindling rebel Army of Northern Virginia had already moved on. But two

FIGURE 28

Long Bridge over the Potomac, viewed from Washington. Unknown photographer. Library of Congress.

The city was heavily fortified throughout the war, being so close to much of the fighting in Virginia. The city was also filled with teamster and ambulance parks, beef on the hoof, hospitals, commissary depots—everything required for the maintenance of a large army.

FIGURE 29

Antietam Bridge, near Sharpsburg, Maryland. Alexander Gardner (Brady Studio). September 1862. Library of Congress.

FIGURE 28

Union soldiers happened upon a small bundle of cigars wrapped in paper lying in the grass. When the paper was unwrapped, it was discovered to be a copy of Lee's battle orders for the entire Maryland campaign. This "Lost Order" was handed over to General McClellan. He didn't entirely believe it could be real but decided to act upon the information anyway.[4]

"We heard all through the war that the army 'was eager to be led against the enemy.' It must have been so, for truthful correspondents said so, and editors confirmed it," wrote an enlisted soldier from New York. "But when you came to hunt for this particular itch, it was always the next regiment that had it."[5] Whether the soldiers were eager to fight or not, whether McClellan believed in the authenticity of the "Lost Order" or not, the fighting would find them all at the town of Sharpsburg on Antietam Creek.

The weather was clear and beautiful on September 16. Alexander Gardner and James Gibson, the Brady team, arrived in Sharpsburg in the wake of Federal regiments, toting a good supply of glass plates, a stereograph camera (for taking 3-D-effect photos), a large box camera, and chemicals in the What-Is-It Wagon. Thus far most of the photographs made by the traveling operators and presented to the public were static, composed images—soldiers in camp, bridges and train trestles, ranks of mounted cavalry standing at attention, artillery emplacements, sentries on picket duty, ambulance parks. So far, "war photography" was a bloodless art. Brady's team was about to change that.

When the battle opened the next day, Lee had approximately 40,000 men under his command; McClellan more than twice that number.[6] Fighting began north of Sharpsburg soon after dawn, with troops moving along the Hagerstown Pike and through the woods, firing as they went. Among the trees the debris of falling leaves, twigs, and branches gave the impression that a fierce storm had suddenly torn loose from the sky.[7] A small church, the modest meetinghouse of a German Baptist pacifist sect, the Dunkers, was on a swell of high ground and therefore the scene of horrific struggle—high ground always gives an offensive advantage. The slaughter at the Dunker Church was unprecedented. "There is nothing to do but advance or break into a rout . . . so we go forward on

FIGURE 29

FIGURE 30
The Dunker Church.
Alexander Gardner. New-
York Historical Society.

the run, heads downward as if under a pelting rain," said a sixteen-year-old Ohio soldier.[8] Confederate General John B. Gordon said later that "this portion of the field was lost and recovered, until the green corn that grew upon it looked as if it had been struck by a storm of bloody hail."[9]

Nearby, a well-worn road that had sunk between high banks over the years was used as an entrenchment by Confederate forces. But it turned into a trap as Union artillery was thrown at it repeatedly, killing so many rebel soldiers that the sunken road acquired a new name: Bloody Lane. The Irish Brigade of the Army of the Potomac held high ground overlooking the sunken road, and was able to enfilade the position until it was stacked up to the banks with corpses.[10] "I was astonished to observe our troops moving along the front and passing over what appeared to be a long, heavy column of the enemy without paying it any attention whatever," remarked an officer on McClellan's staff. "I borrowed a [field]glass from an officer, and discovered this to be actually a column of the enemy's dead and wounded lying along a hollow road . . . [A]mong the prostrate mass I could clearly distinguish the movements of those endeavoring to crawl away from the ground."[11]

A large barn close to the fighting was commandeered as a field hospital, with Union soldiers turning the cattle out of the stalls and laying their wounded comrades on hay that was quickly soaked with blood.[12] The battle continued through the day,

Entered according to Act of Congress, 1r

filling the air with smoke and the screams of dying men and horses and the deafening roar of cannon and musket fire. In the thick haze little was visible but the flash of artillery; each man seemed to be fighting alone in a gray fog of violence and chaos. Occasionally a man was felled by a ramrod shot from a musket in his own ranks, because in the frenzy of loading and ramming, soldiers sometimes forgot to draw the ramrod out and instead shot it like a bolt from a crossbow.[13] Among the artillery units the great guns had to be cooled with wet blankets

862, by Alex. Gardner, in the Clerk's Office of the District Court of the District of Columbia.

FIGURE 30

during the relentless firing,[14] and the gun carriages gouged the ground like plow blades with each shuddering recoil. Gradually, bloodily, with mayhem, violence, and destruction, the superior Union strength beat Lee's forces back—and back, and back—but at terrible cost. At the end of the day the combined casualty count was 26,000 men killed or wounded; it was the bloodiest single day in American history.

Lee withdrew, regrouping and waiting for McClellan to resume the battle, but all of September 18 slipped away while the ever-hesitant McClellan debated his next move. In the night Lee simply took his army into retreat—beaten, but not destroyed.[15] As Lee's forces turned away from Antietam in the darkness, the smoke from campfires and burning barns and haystacks mingled itself with the lingering cloud of gun smoke.[16]

The next morning, as soon as light allowed, Gardner and Gibson got to work.

1861 The War For the Union.

560

11.

THE DEAD OF ANTIETAM

Barely one month later a steady stream of visitors was observed entering and exiting the Brady establishment in New York City. The activity lured more passersby to stop at the door, where a small sign announced that a series of photographs from the war was now on display at Brady's Album Gallery: The Dead of Antietam. Upstairs the exhibition room was filled with silent, awestruck visitors. Some lingered by one image or another, others averted their eyes in haste, only to return and then study the next. There were glass plate prints and stereographs: double photos taken with the two-lens camera that could give a 3-D effect when viewed through a special optical device. Pictures of this sort—the blood still fresh and the bodies still warm (or so it seemed to the shuddering visitors)—had never been shown to the public.

Gardner and Gibson had taken seventy views in the smoky aftermath of Antietam, the first time photographers had been on the scene before the burial details had performed their somber services.[17] Now, amid the hustle and bustle of Broadway, the photographers had brought the war to the public as never before.

"Mr. Brady has done something to bring home to us the terrible reality and earnestness of war," wrote the *New York Times*. "If he has not brought bodies and laid them in our door-yards and along the streets, he has done something very like it. . . . These pictures have a terrible distinctness. . . . We would scarce choose to be in the gallery, when one of the women bending over them should recognize a husband, a son, or a brother in the still, lifeless lines of bodies, that lie ready for the gaping trenches."[18]

The battlefield landmarks already known by name to the public from the newspapers and war dispatches were now presented to their view: the Dunker Church, the Bloody Lane, Hagerstown Pike. Bodies maimed by gunfire and artillery and distorted by rigor mortis seemed to accost the patrons of the Brady gallery: To say the New Yorkers were shocked does not begin to describe the public reaction to the photos. People had been accustomed to seeing portraits of famous

FIGURE 31

The sunken road. Alexander Gardner. Stereograph. New-York Historical Society.

FIGURE 32

Dead: Horse of a Confederate colonel; both killed at Battle of Antietam. Alexander Gardner. Stereograph. New-York Historical Society.

FIGURE 33

Antietam, Confederate dead by a fence on the Hagerstown road. Alexander Gardner. Library of Congress.

FIGURE 31

Entered according to act of Congress, in the year 1862, by Alexander Gardner, in the Clerk's Office of the District Court of the District of Columbia.

FIGURE 32

FIGURE 33

Americans at Brady's; now he was showing them nameless soldiers. And because they were nameless, they could easily have been kin to anyone walking through the gallery with dread and awe. Would the body in the next photograph be a friend, a schoolmate, the son of a neighbor?

What had been remote and unseen for two years was suddenly, horrifically, visible.

FIGURE 34
*Antietam, Md. Bodies
of Confederate dead
gathered for burial.
Alexander Gardner. Sept.
1862. Library of Congress.*

12.

McCLELLAN'S BODYGUARD

In the immediate aftermath of Antietam Lincoln had rejoiced in finally—finally!—having a Union victory to launch his next step. It was exactly what he had been waiting for, waiting for and needing, in order to turn the war into something more meaningful. Within a week newspapers published the preliminary Emancipation Proclamation.[19] Declaring this a war to end slavery meant that now the Confederacy was clearly fighting a war to *preserve* slavery. What had at first been framed as a political argument about the rights of states to control their own laws was suddenly much less abstract, much more stark. Europe, waffling until this point, now could give no thought to supporting the Confederacy, for Europe could not assist in perpetuating slavery.[20] The Confederate States of America were now exiled from the company of civilized nations.

Nevertheless, the war could not be won without defeating Lee's Army of Northern Virginia; yet after his bloody victory at Antietam, McClellan showed no signs of pursuit. The Army of the Potomac remained in Maryland while the fine autumn days ticked by and the best season for fighting grew shorter and shorter.

Lincoln went to visit the army at the start of October with the aim of encouraging McClellan to get on with it. While he reviewed the troops, he found the general full of excuses and rationalizations for not pursuing Lee, surrounded by the army that still outnumbered the Army of Northern Virginia by tens of thousands. Lincoln himself calculated the Union strength under McClellan to be 88,095 men, already reinforced since the battle. "This is General McClellan's bodyguard," Lincoln remarked, and finally sent orders to the general: "The President directs that you cross the Potomac and give battle to the enemy or drive him south. Your army must move now, while the roads are good."[21]

Still McClellan didn't move. He simply defied the president and did not advance, and every day was a gift to General Lee. The middle of October arrived, and a month had passed since the victory at Antietam. "The army was unmovable. It was

FIGURE 35

impatient at this long inaction. The country was astonished at it. Everywhere it was asked, 'What is McClellan doing?'"[22] wrote one commentator.

While New Yorkers gaped at the photographs at Brady's Album Gallery, and *Harper's Weekly* published engravings based on the Antietam views (crediting them to Brady), Lincoln sent telegram after telegram to the motionless McClellan. "I have just read your dispatch about sore-tongued and fatigued horses," he wrote. "Will you pardon me for asking what the horses of your army have done since the battle of Antietam that fatigue anything?"[23]

The next day the Army of the Potomac roused itself and began heading back toward Virginia, but without any urgent sense of pursuing Lee.

On November 5 Lincoln decided that McClellan's terminal case of "the slows"[24] was more than he could tolerate, and he demonstrated just what he thought of the general's lack of get-up-and-go. "By direction of the President, it is ordered that Major General McClellan be relieved from the command of the Army of the Potomac; and that Major General Ambrose Burnside take command of that Army."[25]

FIGURE 36

13.

FREDERICKSBURG, COLD AS DEATH

Because Alexander Gardner had enjoyed a quasi-official relationship with McClellan's staff (attached to the Topographical Engineers with the honorary rank of captain while also working covertly for the Secret Service[26]), the general's dismissal meant that Gardner's access and his responsibilities with the Secret Service were reduced.[27] His role in photographing maps and logistical sites came to an end; and he also chose to end his role as the manager of Brady's Washington gallery. Whether the split was Brady's idea or Gardner's, they agreed at this time to go their separate ways, and Gardner set up his own Washington photography studio and gallery.

Timothy O'Sullivan, one of the most experienced of the Brady field operators, went with him.

Although the operators had been allowed to copyright their photographs under their own names,[28] the prints manufactured by the E. and H. T. Anthony Company all bore the "Photo by Brady" stamp; and the breathtaking Antietam photographs were all credited by public opinion to Mathew Brady. When *Harper's Weekly* copied some of the Antietam photos as engravings, they were described as being "by the well-known and enterprising photographer, Mr. M. B. Brady."[29] The field operators, who had been risking their lives at the heels of the army, had perhaps been nursing a feeling of injustice, whether Brady was at fault or not. Certainly it was in the nature of the studio tradition for Brady to get the credit, but the tradition was beginning to crumble.

Brady did not allow Gardner's departure to affect his own plans; by late November he applied for more financial credit[30] as he continued to pump funds into supplies and equipment for his remaining operators—of whom there were many. Although winter was closing in, it did not appear as though the fighting was quite over for the year, and there were still pictures to be made before the weather got too cold for wet-plate photography. Brady and Gardner teams, now in competition, would continue to work side by side throughout the remainder of the war.

FIGURE 37
Fredericksburg from the river, showing Confederate troops and bridge. Brady Studio. National Archives.

The new commander, General Burnside, was preparing to do battle with Lee's army and had begun a slow buildup of Federal forces across the Rappahannock River from Fredericksburg, Virginia. So slow was the buildup, however, that it gave Lee ample time to secure his defenses in the heights above town, and by the end of November neither army had any secrets from the other—there would be no element of surprise, and the advantage would inevitably go to the army with the better tactical position. Each side could see clearly who was gaining that crucial advantage.

"The narrow river brought the outposts of the armies within speaking distance; and conversations, jokes, newspapers, and tobacco were exchanged by the pickets of the two armies until prohibited," recalled a Union soldier later.[31] Close enough to chat across the picket lines meant close enough to see the faces of the men each would try to kill.

In Washington, Lincoln was rallying support for the Emancipation Proclamation, scheduled to go into effect on January 1, and wrote to Congress: "In giving freedom to the slave, we assure freedom to the free—honorable alike in what we give, and what we preserve. We shall nobly save, or meanly lose, the last, best hope of earth."[32] In early December it was as if the Union were drawing a deep breath before taking a plunge into an unfathomable pool. Big things were about to happen, both politically and militarily.

FIGURE 37

Meanwhile, Lee's artillery now commanded a crucial offensive position overlooking the town of Fredericksburg from a ridge behind it called Marye's Heights. People on both sides of the river were beginning to wonder if Burnside, too, had a case of "the slows," but he was reluctant to cross the river except on pontoons, portable bridges that would allow him to cross in greater numbers than the single narrow bridge the road traversed. But the pontoon equipment wasn't ready, and wasn't there when he needed it, causing delay after delay.[33]

Lee's army urged the residents of Fredericksburg to evacuate before the Union forces began a bombardment. Six thousand frightened civilians took flight, cramming themselves aboard every southbound train and leaving the town nearly deserted.[34] On December 11, with the pontoons finally on hand, Union engineers began throwing the temporary bridges across the Rappahannock; they were repeatedly sniped at by Confederate sharpshooters until Federal artillery commenced shelling the town.

Slowly, division by division, the Union troops began crossing the river into Fredericksburg, until on December 13 they pressed forward on the attack. Lee, from his position on Marye's Heights above town, cast wave upon wave of artillery and musket fire down onto the advancing troops. Throughout the war it was just such assaults that cost the attackers so much: Defensive strength—a high position overlooking a town, for example—simply outweighed a man's ability to walk and shoot. "I wish these people would go away and let us alone," Lee said as the uphill assault continued.[35]

But they would not go away; they would not stop advancing, although entire ranks of men fell like melting snow upon the ground. Somehow, Burnside imagined that superior numbers could make up for such a terrible disadvantage of terrain. It could not.

With temperatures dropping below zero in the frosty December night, the Union succumbed to another miserable defeat.

A PHOTOGRAPH NOT TAKEN

December 13, 1862: Fredericksburg. Night. Overhead, waving like bunting, is the aurora borealis, seldom seen so far south, perhaps a sign of Divine approval for the outcome of the battle. Tomorrow is Sunday, and preachers will speculate whether the Creator had a hand in the Union defeat. On the field clouds of breath appear at the pale lips of the mortally wounded men: They breathe shallowly, shivering, the flickering aurora reflected in their dimming eyes. Among them pick survivors, searching for good boots, warm socks, a knitted scarf. These men on the ground will not need them anymore. A soldier leans down, his bare hand outstretched to take something from the breast of a fallen foe, but the man is not dead yet; he reaches up his own pale and trembling hand, clutches the scavenger's wrist, whispers urgently, "Please."

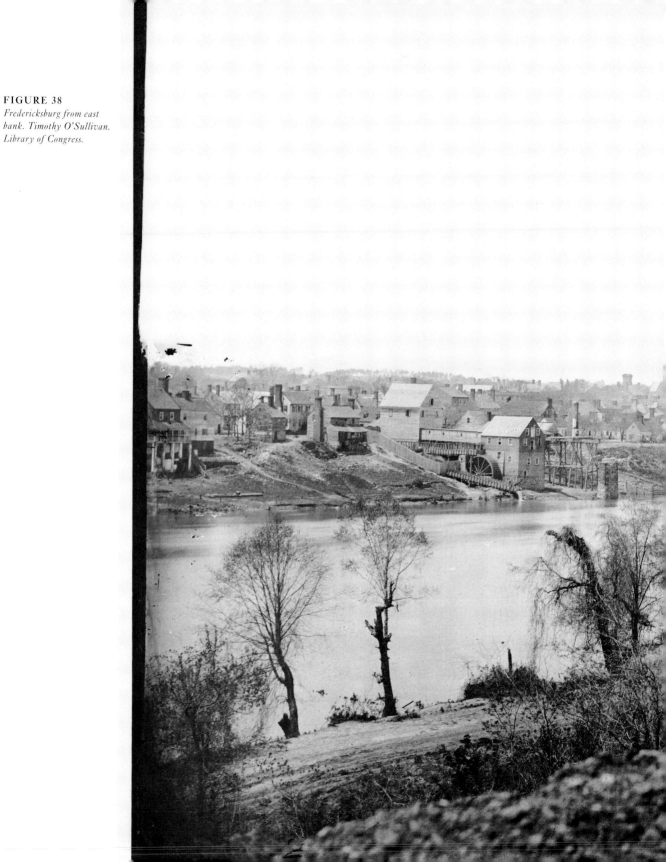

FIGURE 38
*Fredericksburg from east
bank. Timothy O'Sullivan.
Library of Congress.*

A PHOTOGRAPH NOT TAKEN

January 1, 1863: Boston. Gulls from the harbor wheel overhead against a white sky. On Beacon Hill the mansions of merchant dynasties that made their fortunes in the Triangle Trade are still festooned with Yuletide garlands, and the doors open and shut on bundled visitors while cries of "Happy New Year" bounce off the iced cobblestones. The Proclamation is being read aloud to a great crowd of white and black, standing shoulder to shoulder in the frosty air. Tears glisten on cheeks both light and dark, and hands are clasped in prayers of Thanksgiving. Frederick Douglass, the great orator and abolitionist, the dauntless rebuker of the president, listens with them. His face is dark skinned, his hair swept back from a broad brow, his expression unreadable. Is it fierce triumph? Is it righteous anger that it has taken so long? Is it sorrow for the slaves not included in this proclamation, the slaves of the loyal border states that have remained in the Union and are therefore not in rebellion? His expression says: This is only a partial Jubilee. We are not finished, Lord. We are not yet finished in our work.

14.

THE YEAR OF THE TURNING POINT BEGINS

On Christmas Day, 1862, President and Mrs. Lincoln visited soldiers in hospitals in and around the capital. Sentries paced outside the White House.[36] The city was filled with the casualties of Fredericksburg, and men continued to die of their wounds, or of dysentery and typhoid fever, bronchitis or diarrhea.[37] Medical care was far from expert. Volunteer nurse Walt Whitman described an untrained orderly in a hospital treating an unlucky patient: "[The] wardmaster gave him inwardly muriate of ammonia, intended for a wash for his feet."[38] Soldiers died in agony every day. The presence of so much pain and death threw January 1, 1863 (a day greeted by so many with joy), into stark contrast. The Emancipation Proclamation, so long anticipated, went into effect on the first day of the year. Lincoln did not know if his army would accept the war as a war to free the slaves.

The Army of the Potomac was resting and nursing its wounds in winter camp, but fighting continued in the western theater of the war—in Tennessee and Missouri,

Arkansas and Mississippi. In late January the Union troops in Virginia attempted to get themselves moving again for a winter campaign; soldiers were instructed to leave everything but their campaigning gear behind, and the camp was soon littered with checkerboards, baseball bats, furniture, banjos, and anything else too heavy to carry.[39] But the great army was soon hopelessly stuck by mud so thick that horses and mules died of exhaustion trying to pull wagons and artillery.[40] The army was forced to return to its winter camp and wait for better weather.

The camps were muddy hodgepodges of log shanties in all sizes and shapes. Makeshift hearths made from dismantled stone walls and brick chimneys caught fire from time to time,[41] or a shanty would collapse into the mud. Corduroy roads—roads made of saplings and logs laid side by side—connected the parts of camp to one another. The miserable "Mud March" had put everyone into a foul temper, and rain fell incessantly. It was an unhappy winter for many. They were a mere fifty miles from Washington, and yet the men were dying of scurvy because army rations were so bad and so badly distributed.[42]

February 10 found Mathew Brady far from the mud of Virginia: In New York City, he acted as portrait photographer to the celebrity wedding of General Tom Thumb to Lavinia Warren and sold *carte de visite* copies of the "Fairy Wedding Party" portrait. The wedding itself was a media event, and P. T. Barnum (for whom Tom Thumb worked) sold tickets for seventy-five dollars each.[43] Profits from the wedding portrait

copies, presumably, went to help support Brady's war photography mission.

Yet there was nothing much to photograph at the moment—not in the war, at any rate. Men of the Irish Brigade celebrated St. Patrick's Day in winter camp at Falmouth, Virginia, with boxing and sack races and greased-pole climbing;[44] the weather remained chilly into April. Life in the Army of the Potomac was dreary and depressing. So far the great war to preserve the cause of freedom was a disappointment, and soldiers knew, when officers' wives began to be regular visitors at camp, that

FIGURE 39

Gen. Tom Thumb and Bride
Feb. 13th, 1863

FIGURE 40

there was no likelihood of moving ahead. "It is not our fault, good friends, that we are not at work," wrote a private. "The Lord knows we are anxious to finish the job as soon as possible and return to our heart–loved homes."[45]

Lincoln, too, was frustrated with inaction. "Our prime object is the enemies' army in front of us, and is not with, or about, Richmond,"[46] he warned General Joseph Hooker—yet another new commander. Readying for an assault against Richmond was pointless as long as Lee's army remained at large. The only way to win the war was to engage Lee and keep engaging him in order to wear him down, bringing the sheer weight of superior numbers and resources to the job. The North had more men, more money, more factories, more arms, more ships, more food, more *everything* than the Confederacy—sooner or later that would have to count for *something,* but it wouldn't happen if the Union sat motionless in Falmouth, and it wouldn't happen with commanders who hesitated.

What Lincoln needed most, more than the moral high ground, more than popular support, more than a resounding battlefield victory here or there, was a general who was ready and willing to *fight.*

FIGURE 41
Camp scene showing winter
huts and corduroy roads.
Brady Studio. National
Archives.

FIGURE 41

A PHOTOGRAPH NOT TAKEN

Winter camp, Falmouth, very early morning, just after reveille has been sounded. Men are dragging themselves from their tents and shacks, straightening with difficulty, and coughing resounds from one end of the camp to another. Smoke from hundreds of cook fires rises straight up in the cold, still air. The mascot of a Connecticut regiment, a black-spotted pig, is snuffling behind a sutler's wagon, where a pile of discarded apples too wormy even for soldiers to pay for has frozen into a solid block. Now another noise joins the coughing: a strange clanking, grinding din that is growing louder by the moment. Thousands of men are pounding coffee beans with their rifle butts inside tin pots and pails. It sounds like the tramping of soldiers in armor, looks like the working pistons of some sprawling machine.

15.

THE WILDERNESS: PART ONE

"Fighting Joe" Hooker was at the head of the Army of the Potomac now, and as April ended, he put that army into motion, crossing the Rapahannock upriver from Fredericksburg.[47] A sizable force of Confederate troops still held Fredericksburg, and so Union divisions moved to flank the town through an area known locally as the Wilderness, an expanse of dense, thickety woods, tangled with brambles and vines. Skirmishes flared up like brushfires. Small settlements, usually named after whatever family had built there first, made clearings here and there in the greenery. For his headquarters Hooker chose the home of the Chancellor family, at the crossroads called Chancellorsville. Regiments began to mass around Chancellorsville, and Hooker wrote confident telegrams to the president.

Lee moved to block off the roads leading out of the Wilderness toward Richmond, and on May 1 the Battle of Chancellorsville commenced. Like other Union commanders before him, Hooker seemed daunted by Lee and, despite greater strength, gave up the offensive. Again Lee controlled the

fighting. May 3: "We have had a desperate fight yesterday and today which has resulted in no success to us having lost a position of two lines which has been selected for our defence," a no-longer-confident Hooker telegraphed to Lincoln. "We will endeavor to do our best. My troops are in good spirits. We have fought desperately today. No general ever commanded a more devoted army."[48] In the Chancellor house the piano in the sitting room was used as an amputation table[49] while the ground shook with repeated detonations of artillery and mortar fire. Blazes erupted in the dense underbrush of the Wilderness, and swiftly moving forest fires finished the wounded men who lay upon the ground; afterward, they could be identified only by turning them over to examine the unburned parts of their uniforms,[50] and soldiers reported hearing a wounded whippoorwill crying above the sobs and moans of dying men.[51] At one point, while Hooker stood on the porch to survey the action, the house was shelled and a falling porch column knocked the general unconscious.

FIGURE 42
Confederate dead behind a stone wall, Marye's Heights. May 1863. National Archives.

FIGURE 43
Marye's Heights, Fredericksburg. Confederate caisson and eight horses destroyed by a 32-lb. shell from second Mass. siege gun. Brady Studio. May 3, 1863. National Archives.

The battle continued for three days, with action again at Marye's Heights in nearby Fredericksburg, and along the Rappahannock. The first battle at Fredericksburg, in December, had been too cold to allow for photography. Now the mild May weather let the photographers record the effects of battle during a temporary halt in the firing to allow stretcher bearers onto the field. Timothy O'Sullivan was there, as were the Brady operators. The photographs they brought home were of ruined rebel positions and men, but the battle was not a Union victory. Once again, through boldness and quick action, Lee had prevailed, and once again a Union general had failed to rout the rebel army. Lincoln began to get word from corps and division commanders that they were not entirely confident of Hooker's ability to lead the Army of the Potomac. For the rest of May and into June both armies remained along the

FIGURE 42

FIGURE 43

Rappahannock, with additional skirmishes and small engagements. By June 10 Hooker suggested to Lincoln that it was a good time to head for Richmond, to which the frustrated president replied, "I think Lee's Army and not Richmond is your true objective point . . . Fight him when opportunity offers. If he stays where he is, fret him, and fret him."[52] So fighting continued in Virginia, with men dropping from heat exhaustion by the sides of the road and the residents of Washington nervously glancing out their windows as the sound of distant cannon fire reached them on the warm air. Lee was beginning to probe toward the west and north, sniffing along the edge of Pennsylvania, and from his office in the White House Lincoln cast about for a more aggressive general, like a hunter wandering in the wilderness searching for his hound.

A PHOTOGRAPH NOT TAKEN

Somewhere in the valley of the Ohio, early May: Apple blossoms have turned the countryside white, as if a late snow had powdered the rolling landscape. Underfoot, along well-trodden cow paths, grow medicinal herbs—pennyroyal, horehound, mullein. As far as the eye can see are Johnny Appleseed trees, giving their glory to the sky with outstretched limbs, beautiful mature trees spreading in sweet-scented waves across a beautiful green land. They are home to birds, shelter to deer, delight of bees. The apple groves cross borders, straddle boundaries, offer fruit to all, just like the man who planted them. His voice, saying, "Good news, straight from Heaven," still echoes faintly among the rustling boughs and shakes a thousand petals loose to flutter to the ground.

A PHOTOGRAPH NOT TAKEN

Somewhere in south Texas. Heat mirages create false pools of water on the baked plain, where a woman weeps beside a dying mule; blood oozes from a deep puncture wound in its side, and it groans heavily. Between her and her shanty is the wild longhorn steer that gored her only animal; these cattle have been breeding in the sagebrush for two hundred years, since the days of the Spanish missions when Apache raids chased rancheros away and forced them to abandon their cows. Now the mesquite and sage are teeming with cattle, and the steers are as jumpy as antelope and as mean as hornets. The one between the homesteader and her house paws the ground, catching the odor of the mule's blood on the hot, shimmering air. There is nothing this woman can do but wait for the steer to go away; her only firearm is an old buffalo gun her husband left with her when he enlisted for the Confederate cause, but it is too heavy for her and besides, she has no ammunition. She has to wait beside the dying mule, weeping with rage and despair. She just has to wait.

16.

HIGH TIDE

All the plates exposed during the winter and spring campaigns had been printed by late June. Brady and Gardner were busy in their separate Washington galleries, filling orders for prints and continuing their *carte de visite* operations.[53] Freshly recruited regiments continued to pour into Washington: The draft act signed by Lincoln the previous year had spurred enlistments, and there was no shortage of young men looking to get their images in uniform recorded.

Even as the new recruits were having their portraits taken, Lee was making yet another bold move. He had concluded that the only way to defend the South was by invading the North; if there was fighting north of Washington, public opinion in the Union states might change swiftly.[54] So far, with fighting mainly in Virginia and the far-off western front, the war was a popular thing among citizens of the North. It hadn't really touched them directly. Of course, many families had lost beloved sons and brothers, but Union farms and factories continued with business as usual, towns and railroads were unharmed. Seaports still shipped their goods to foreign ports. Business was good, and having a sense of moral superiority made the whole thing that much more worthy. It was easy to be in favor of the war when it cost the average Northern family so little. But if the war were actually to *hurt*, hurt the way it hurt in the South, then maybe it wouldn't be such a popular affair and the citizens would cry out to President Lincoln to call it off.

Lee made for Pennsylvania.

"We expect more hard marching," a Union private wrote in his diary, "but shall either get toughened to it, or as the boys say, die toughening."[55]

News of the Confederate advance sent families in the southern part of Pennsylvania scurrying northward, away from the relentless Virginia general.[56] In Washington, Lincoln replaced General Hooker with General George Gordon Meade as commander of the Army of the Potomac. Meade was surprised at this unexpected and unasked-for responsibility, but hastened to do something about Lee's Army of Northern Virginia. Within three days

FIGURE 44

of assuming command, Meade met the invading Confederates at Gettysburg, Pennsylvania, seventy-five miles from the U.S. capital.

It started as a skirmish, as Confederate foragers coming into town from west of Gettysburg ran into Union cavalry. Both armies had been moving their great lines of men and equipment through the Pennsylvania countryside, neither really sure where the other was. No general had chosen Gettysburg as a battleground, but circumstances decided otherwise. The skirmish developed into a full-scale engagement, with reinforcements hurrying up from the rear on both sides. Civilians standing on their front porches while the arriving troops marched by ladled out cups of water for thirsty Federal soldiers. Some townsfolk ignored orders to hide in their cellars; some retreated in dismay as fighting erupted volcanically all around them.[57]

July 1 ended with the Confederates holding an advantage, and General Lee was riding on a high tide of success that looked as though it might carry the cause of secession once and for all. But when the second day of battle got underway, there was no clear advantage on either side: Slaughter was equally enormous for both armies.

A bell atop a farmhouse was struck again and again by bullets, adding its hollow note to the roar of artillery.[58] "I thought I had become hardened to almost anything," wrote a soldier afterward. "But I cannot say I ever wish to see another sight like that I saw on the battlefield of Gettysburg."[59]

The country waited for news. "We are here still on tiptoe with all eyes turned toward the Northwest where I have felt all day that a mortal combat was going on for our country's life," wrote a Washington woman in her diary.[60]

By the third of July, news of the collision of the armies was finally reaching the home front. Gardner and his team—O'Sullivan and Gibson—prepared to leave Washington as soon as possible with two What-Is-It Wagons,[61] while Lee made another of his usual audacious moves. This time, however, the gamble did not pay off. He had become accustomed to beating long odds, and he was confident his troops could do whatever he asked of them, but he was about to make the same mistake that Burnside had made at Fredericksburg: sending troops uphill against entrenched positions.[62] To begin, he opened a bombardment of artillery against the Union position in the local cemetery, using 138 field guns for an hour and a half, the largest artillery bombardment of the war. "Holes like graves were gouged in the earth by exploding shells. The flowers in bloom upon the graves at the Cemetery were shot

FIGURE 45

away," a Union private wrote. "Tombs and monuments were knocked to pieces, and ordinary gravestones shattered in rows."[63] Then Lee, believing the Union resistance to have softened, sent 15,000 soldiers under the command of General George E. Pickett to attack the center of the Federal line. Pickett's Charge threw men into a hurricane of artillery and musket fire that mowed them down by the hundreds. It was a military catastrophe, and a loss that Lee could not afford; the tide turned, and the Fourth of July dawned with the Confederate army in retreat, followed by an ambulance wagon train some seventeen miles long.[64]

Independence Day was marked throughout the North with wild jubilation. Placards on bulletin boards outside the newspaper offices read "Glorious Victory for the Union Army!" and bells pealed their hallelujahs throughout Washington. Revelers shot off their pistols, and children ran screaming with excitement through the streets.[65] Lincoln watched the fireworks from the White House that evening, lamenting that Meade had chosen not to pursue Lee and put an end to the war.[66]

In Gettysburg, rain was falling on ground trampled into bloody mud. A Union drummer boy "went out on the battlefield. An awful sight, men, horses, all lying in heaps as far as the eye can see."[67] Souvenir hunters were already combing the ground when Gardner and his team arrived with a large plate camera and a stereographic camera.[68] Overcast skies, mist, and a relent-

Entered according to Act of Congress, in t

less drizzle lowered the light so much that exposure times were the sheerest guesswork; there was precious little daylight to waste.[69] Gardner had caused a sensation with his Antietam pictures, and if he was to duplicate that triumph (and this time get the credit for it), he had to get his photos made before the burial parties removed all the dead.

The fact that the grave details were working quickly forced the Gardner team to be creative. With each exposure requiring an average of ten minutes, they could not hope to cover the entire battlefield—

by Alex. Gardner, in the Clerk's Office of the District Court of the District of Columbia.

FIGURE 46

moving the What-Is-It Wagons would use up time better spent making pictures, so they did most of their work in the same two locations.[70] They took approximately sixty photographs, often shooting the same bodies from different angles and, when necessary, moving bodies to create a more tragic picture. Nobody would have been surprised or shocked to know it, either. The art of photography required that the picture create the most moving effect, and if that meant posing the bodies of the dead, that was appropriate. It didn't alter the most basic truth about the images—that they were pictures of war's fatal power.

Gardner and his team got the vivid and heart-wrenching photographs he was looking for, and yet his quick arrival worked against him. By photographing the battleground before a full account of the battle was made, he missed photographing the most important landmarks. His pictures moved the heart, but they could not illustrate three days of epic struggle. Brady, arriving after Gardner's team left, would be the one to take those pictures.

FIXIN
THE

G IMAGE

THE WAR FOR THE UNION.

17.

GETTYSBURG BY BRADY

Mathew Brady did not arrive at the battlefield until July 15, a week and a half after the Gardner team. The burial parties had carried out their work; there were no more gruesome casualties to photograph in their heartrending poses of death and quick decay. What Brady did do, however, was tour the site with local guides. In a week and a half the stories of that mighty struggle on the three first days of July had become common lore in the United States, and Brady was ready to provide the illustrations for the epic. Places that a month before had been known only to locals were now local to all Americans: Little Round Top and Big Round Top, the Peach Orchard, Culp's Hill and Devil's Den, Seminary Ridge, McPherson's Woods.

Brady and his assistants made approximately thirty photographs at Gettysburg, and fair weather smiled on his efforts, giving his images a crispness that Gardner's photos—for all their grim drama—did not have.[1] With the aid of his local guides he covered the major sites, showing panoramic vistas of the settings for each part of the three-day battle. Because the bodies had long since been buried, he was faced with the task of turning the scene into something quieter, more reflective. His photographs have the look of landscape paintings, and seem to say, "Here is the ground where history was made." Every site already famous from the newspaper accounts of the war was photographed by the Brady team, and because of this, it was the Brady photographs that appeared in the August 1863 issue of Harper's Weekly to illustrate the story of the battle, and not Gardner's pictures.[2] "Mr. Brady, the photographer, to whose industry and energy we are indebted for many of the most reliable war pictures, has been to Gettysburg battlefield and executed a number of photographs of what he saw there," wrote the editors.[3] The magazine devoted its entire issue to engravings made from Brady's Gettysburg photographs.

Brady himself appears (wearing his trademark straw hat) in many of the photographs, often looking away into the distance in a contemplative pose, as though offering a quiet prayer on behalf of the dead—or on

FIGURE 47

FIGURE 48

behalf of the ideals the war was being fought for. Placing himself in the photos had two important effects that set his pictures apart from Gardner's post-battle images. The Brady photos feature living figures rather than dead bodies. After the carnage of the battle depicted by Gardner, the message these photos sends to the viewer is life, continuity, hope, salvation. In other words, this war is not only about death, but is also about life going on after the gun smoke has cleared. Further, placing himself in the pictures guaranteed that the public would associate Brady with these epic scenes. *Photo by Brady*. The Civil War, brought to you in black and white by the celebrated Mathew B. Brady of Broadway and Washington. It gave additional support to the idea already in the public mind that Brady was some-

how single-handledly responsible for all the war photographs they'd been seeing.[4] Over the years, many—if not most—of the most famous Gettysburg photographs, including Gardner's, were attributed to Brady, simply because his was the name fixed in history's memory.[5]

FIGURE 49

GETTYSBURG BY BRADY **99**

A PHOTOGRAPH NOT TAKEN

Fort Zachary Taylor, Key West, Florida, late afternoon: A warm wet wind stirs the fronds of the palms, rattling them together with a sound like muskets falling in a heap, or a saber salute. By the big Columbiad cannons, whose three-mile range is the scourge of Confederate ships, Union gunners stand smoking cigars and looking up at the sky. The horizon is a strange greenish gray, and whitecaps are beginning to show out on the water. There—there is a steamship struggling against the wind, the smoke from its funnels buffeting one way and then another. The gunners watch quietly, the smoke from their cigars whipping away on the breath of the coming storm. Fat drops of rain begin splatting onto the barrel of the cannon, and the palm trees shake their blades again in wild warning.

18.

REDEDICATION

The Brady and Gardner teams remained in the Gettysburg area for days, continuing to make photographs. With the Union victory in Pennsylvania, Lee's army was in no shape for serious fighting, and the eastern theater of the war quieted down, dogs lying low in the summer heat; Lee crossed back into Virginia on July 13, with Meade's army in slow pursuit. Action continued in the west, where the Mississippi River had finally come completely under Federal control. "The Father of Waters again goes unvexed to the sea," said Lincoln.[6]

On July 30 Lincoln signed the Order of Retaliation, which stated that any act of barbarity or unlawful execution by the Confederacy against a captured black soldier (free blacks and escaped slaves were now fighting for the Union) would be met with the execution of a captured rebel soldier; any black soldier sent into slavery in the rebel states would sentence a captured rebel soldier to hard labor.[7] Lincoln sensed that the tide had indeed turned, that the cause of Union would prevail, and that the army was ready to rededicate itself.

That summer Lincoln's son Tad often rode his pony by the side of the president's carriage.[8] In Washington people had grown accustomed to seeing the huge derrick swinging its great arm above the dome of the Capitol, steadily building the nation while the army fought to preserve it.[9] In late August Federal gunboats began a bombardment of Fort Sumter, pounding it into rubble; the rebel forces garrisoned inside doggedly shored up the ruins and refused to surrender, but the navy was relentless.[10]

Throughout the fall, action continued in the west in the Mississippi River region, and skirmishes and small battles sparked and flared throughout Virginia. Meade was trying to turn Lee toward Richmond, but without success.

And back in Gettysburg plans were well underway for the dedication ceremonies for the battlefield cemetery, to be held on November 19. In the few short months since July, the site had acquired an epic status for the North. The formal opening of the cemetery, where thousands of soldiers from every state in the Union lay buried with

FIGURE 50

their comrades, was expected to draw spectators by the thousands. On the schedule was a fine speech by a great orator, former Senator Edward Everett, and there would be military music and a dedicatory prayer. The president was scheduled to address the crowd with a few remarks as well.

As the day of the ceremony neared, Fort Sumter was still under heavy bombardment. In Tennessee, Knoxville was under siege, and Chattanooga was under partial siege as well. Much of Arkansas had fallen under Union control. On November 18 Gettysburg was filled with crowds; Lincoln and his secretaries arrived by train in the evening. The next day, after a two-hour speech by Everett, the president rose from his seat on the platform to say his few words about the dedication of the burial ground. Wounded veterans of the battle, politicians, and citizens from all over the east huddled under a gray November sky, breaking into the president's address several times with polite applause.

"Fourscore and seven years ago our fathers brought forth upon this continent a new nation, conceived in liberty, and dedicated to the proposition that all men are created equal," the president began. "Now we are engaged in a great civil war, testing whether that nation or any nation so conceived and so dedicated can long endure. We are met on a great battlefield of that war. We have come to dedicate a portion of that field as a final resting place for those who here gave their lives that that nation might live. It is altogether fitting and proper that we should do this. But in a larger sense we cannot dedicate, we cannot consecrate, we cannot hallow this ground. The brave men, living and dead, who struggled here, have consecrated it far above our poor power to add or detract. The world will little note nor long remember what we say here, but it can never forget what they did here. It is for us, the living, rather to be dedicated here to the unfinished work which they who fought

FIGURE 51

here have thus far so nobly advanced. It is rather for us to be here dedicated to the great task remaining before us—that from these honored dead we take increased devotion to that cause for which they here gave the last full measure of devotion—that we here highly resolve that these dead shall not have died in vain, that this nation, under God, shall have a new birth of freedom; and that government of the people, by the people, for the people, shall not perish from the earth."

There was more applause as the president resumed his seat on the platform, and then the ceremony was over. The Gettysburg cemetery had been dedicated. And the war had been rededicated—to freedom. To government by the people. To the cause of liberty and equality.

Lincoln's Gettysburg Address was so brief that none of the photographers on hand had finished setting up their cameras with fresh collodion plates; not a single photograph exists of the president giving one of the most important speeches in American history.

A PHOTOGRAPH NOT TAKEN

Camp Drum, Los Angeles: Christmas Eve, 1863. Three boys with lariats are standing in the shadow of a livery stable. Each elbows the others; there are urgent gestures and much pointing toward the paddock. One boy is shoved: He stumbles forward and then springs back into the shadows like a jackrabbit. Lying folded up like strange idle contraptions are the camels used to transport supplies from one military post to another in dry coastal California. The boys have dared one another to rustle a camel for their church nativity service; less daring boys have been sent for a burro, two sheep, and a milk cow. Another child has offered to bring a large pet toad and been ridiculed for his suggestion. From the darkness an ovenbird cries, "Teacher! Teacher!" The camels turn their heads and gaze through long-lashed eyes at the boys in the shadows; one of the animals lets out a horrific grunt, and the boys flee, dropping their lassos in the dirt.

FIGURE 52

19.

THE MAN WE HAVE ALL BEEN LOOKING FOR

Leap Day, February 29, 1864: Lincoln gave his approval for an Act of Congress reviving the rank of lieutenant general, a rank never held before except in an honorary capacity. The lieutenant general of the Union forces would command action both east and west, creating a unified strategy that would—with luck and skill and steady pounding—result in a final defeat for the Confederacy.

The man to be nominated was U. S. Grant. Throughout the first years of war he'd been doggedly pursuing the enemy in the western theater, along the Mississippi and points between the great river and the Appalachian Mountains. He'd been low on swagger, quick to fight, and ready and willing to keep the pressure on. In other words, Ulysses S. ("Unconditional Surrender") Grant was a general who got results, a general who did not let his foe walk away. His description of the art of war was a simple one: The task was "to find out where your enemy is, get at him as soon as you can and strike him as hard as you can, and keep moving on."[11]

He was the man Lincoln had been look-

ing for, a fighting general and maybe even a match for General Lee. By March 3 Grant was on his way from the western theater to Washington to meet the government of the people and receive his commission.

News of Grant's promotion caused a stir as people awaited his command of the Army of the Potomac.[12] Rumors flew through Washington that a violent sweep through Virginia was at the top of his agenda.[13] But mostly people were curious about the general from Ohio. He was a West Pointer but hadn't had a particularly distinguished career until the war began—it wasn't until his victories in the west that anyone had taken note of him. Now everyone was looking forward to seeing him, and they pinned their hopes for success against Lee on the hero of Fort Donelson.

Brady had seen one of the few existing photographs of the general and appointed himself the welcoming committee. On March 8 he went to the train station to look for Grant. A bearded man in a disheveled major general's uniform stepped off the train, and Brady hurried forward to introduce himself and to recommend Willard's Hotel as a good place to stay—and to make a suggestion.

FIGURE 53

"General, the desire to obtain your portrait is so universal I hope you will favor me with a sitting as early as you conveniently can."

Grant replied, "Certainly. I go away tomorrow at one o'clock and must pay my respects to the President and Secretary of War, but after that I promise I will give you a chance."[14]

Brady had scored a triumph. The next day, while the new lieutenant general was formally given his new rank in a White House ceremony, preparations were underway at the Brady studio to take as many photographs as time would allow. Assistants readied four cameras, poised like gunners on an ironclad warship—but one o'clock came and went, and there was no sign of Grant. The feeble March daylight was quickly fading when, at four o'clock, the new commander of the Union forces arrived in a rush at the Brady studio for his sitting. An assistant hurried to the roof to adjust the skylight shades and let in the greatest amount of light; he accidentally broke one of the panes of glass, sending a shower of dagger-sharp chunks of glass down around Grant—who did not flinch.[15] The photograph was made, and the general departed for Virginia for his first look at the Army of the Potomac.

He then returned to Tennessee to confer with General William Tecumseh Sherman and announced by telegram, "Headquarters will be in the field, and until further orders, will be with the Army of the Potomac."[16] Then back he went again to Virginia to look for General Robert E. Lee and start battering away.

On March 23 there was a snowball skirmish in camp near Brandy Station, Virginia,[17] and a feeling of uncertainty about the new commander. "Well, you have never met Bobby Lee and his boys," or "Mind you, Bobby Lee is just over the Rapidan," muttered the veterans in camp, as if they were speaking to the general himself.[18] The soldiers who had enlisted in 1861 for a three-year term of service were due to be mustered out, and Grant needed to gain their trust and encourage them to reenlist.[19] Would he turn out to be another McClellan? Another Burnside? Another Hooker? Another Meade?

He would soon show them what kind of general he was.

FIGURE 54

A PHOTOGRAPH NOT TAKEN

The Wilderness, May 6, 1864: A soldier is lying on his side in the shelter of a heavy, moss-covered log, reloading his weapon. The smoke is so thick, he cannot see the men of his company any longer or hear their voices through the ceaseless barrage of gunfire. Something nudges the back of his leg, and he jerks away instinctively while ramming in the cartridge. The same thing touches him again, and he looks behind him with a scowl: Two cottontail rabbits are huddled in the crook of his knees, staring and rigid with terror. Wondering, he puts out his hand, touches both small soft animals, thinks of his two young children at home, and begins to cry so hard that tears streak through the soot and gunpowder on his cheeks, washing him clean.

20.

THE WILDERNESS: PART TWO

In the dark hours between May 3 and May 4, the Army of the Potomac began moving toward that bristly stretch of Virginia called the Wilderness that it had fought through just one year earlier. And although so near to Richmond, the objective was the Army of Northern Virginia, and not the Confederate capital. At all costs Grant was determined to destroy Lee.[20] At the same time, General Sherman began to lead his forces from Tennessee down into Georgia.

Grant's army was slowed by the immense wagon trains, carrying supplies, that snaked along behind marching troops for miles and had to be protected from raiders.[21] But slow or not, they met Lee's army in the Wilderness on May 5 and 6, amid the heavy underbrush, whipping vines, ravines, streams, and bogs. While Grant whittled and smoked cigars at headquarters, 100,000 Federal troops engaged 60,000 Confederates. A "war of attrition" is one in which both parties keep fighting until one side has simply lost all its strength and has no one left standing. With the numbers in Grant's favor, he could afford to keep throwing his troops at Lee's smaller army—and he did. Losses in the Wilderness were enormous but did not make Grant hesitate or pull back, in spite of warnings from his officers about the wily Lee. "I am heartily sick of hearing about what Lee is going to do," he replied. "Some of you always seem to think he is suddenly going to turn a double somersault, and land in our rear and on both of our flanks at the same time. Go back to your command, and try to think what we are going to do ourselves, instead of what Lee is going to do."[22]

On their way through the woods to pick up the wounded, stretcher bearers carried boxes of musket cartridges to hand over to fighting soldiers.[23] The dense canopy of trees and vines and leaves trapped the smoke, cutting visibility down to almost nothing. Artillery was useless among the dense thickets and couldn't be moved into any kind of position anyway,[24] so it was mainly a musket fight. Bullets flew so thickly that one soldier said, "I could have caught a pot full of them if I had a strong iron vessel rigged on a pole as a butterfly net."[25]

FIGURE 55

FIGURE 55
The Wilderness. Brady Studio. National Archives.

FIGURE 56
Spotsylvania Court House, Va. Burial of a soldier. Timothy O'Sullivan. May 1864. Library of Congress.
For a few days Grant made his headquarters here, and a flock of chickens pecked busily around the building, ignoring the flying bullets.

FIGURE 57
View of North Anna, Va.: Soldiers swimming during a rare break in fighting. Timothy O'Sullivan. May 1864. Stereograph. New-York Historical Society.

And, just as earlier at Chancellorsville, the scrubby underbrush of the Wilderness caught fire, burning wounded men where they lay.[26] Stacks of knapsacks men had piled against logs burned too,[27] leaving men without any of their own possessions (if they left the battle in possession of their lives).

It was to continue this way for most of May: continuous fighting, both armies moving, attacking, digging in positions, jockeying for room in the wooded, rough terrain. In driving rain or clinging fog there was hand-to-hand fighting, bayoneting, clubbing with muskets, the dead and wounded trampled into the muck underfoot.[28] This was May in the Wilderness in little crossroads towns like Spotsylvania Court House and Massaponax Church.

"We digged, we tramped; we tramped, chopped wood and digged," said a soldier from Maine. "It was shovel and shoot, shoot, shovel and dig. We dug before reveille, and fought before noon; marched a short distance, and if it weren't good shooting, piled up the ground."[29] Grant's losses were staggering, but he could afford it—replacements from the North were plentiful, Union cities were still bursting with unenlisted men. Casualties were so routine now that soldiers had taken to writing their names on pieces of paper and pinning them to their coats before going to the front, so their bodies could be identified.[30]

Said a Southern soldier, "We have met a man this time, who either does not know when he is whipped, or who cares not if he loses his whole Army."[31]

It seemed as though Grant didn't; but in fact he knew, and General Lee knew, that if they kept this up long enough, it would be Lee who ran out of soldiers. There wasn't an able-bodied man in the South who wasn't already in the army. It was only a matter of weeks before the Confederate Congress in Richmond authorized boys of seventeen and eighteen and men of between forty-five and fifty for military service. And the South was running out of ammunition, too. Many of the soldiers arriving from the Wilderness at the hospitals in Washington had suffered buckshot wounds, not bullet holes.[32] Lee himself was feeling the pinch and spent more and more time at the front, urging on his troops, who clamored for him to get back, keep safely away. "Lee to the rear!"[33] they yelled when he strayed too close to danger, knowing that if they had any chance, it was only with him as their general. The image of Robert E. Lee as savior of the Confederacy was fixed in every soldier's mind.

FIGURE 57

The Army of the Potomac was getting a very clear picture of its new lieutenant general. "There was no nonsense, no sentiment; only a plain business man of the republic," one of Grant's officers said.[34] His business was making war against General Lee, and pushing the Confederate troops back, toward the South and toward Richmond. No longer was the Army of the Potomac an oversized and underused force with a case of the slows. The hospitals in Washington were becoming so crowded that wounded officers were being billeted in private homes.[35] The wounded kept streaming in from Grant's steadily moving front line. The lieutenant general's strategy was simple: Fight and keep fighting and then keep fighting more. Lee was on the defensive now. Virginia in May had become the wilderness of total war.

FIGURE 56

21.

THE IMAGE OF HISTORY

The number of photographs of the Wilderness Campaign by Timothy O'Sullivan shows that Alexander Gardner's operators were hard at work. Mathew Brady's team was as well, with the boss himself on hand in Virginia in the middle of June.[36] Temporary headquarters (and they were all temporary, with Grant constantly on the move) at Cold Harbor gave Brady a chance to photograph the commander again.

The weather was unspeakably hot, and the louse-plagued soldiers took to calling Cold Harbor Hot Harbor.[37] The entire region seemed to be shrouded with a stench of death; there was no letup. Back in Washington churches were being converted to hospitals as the fighting began to skirt around Richmond, forcing Lee to defend his capital.

Now Petersburg, Virginia, south of Richmond, came under siege in an effort to isolate the capital from the rest of the South by cutting the railroad lines. With Union troops digging in positions around Petersburg, artillery began a steady bombardment. Before he left Virginia, Brady took a few more photographs to round out his collection. Again he himself appears in many of the photographs: It was his assistants who operated the camera, Brady who selected the views and arranged the compositions. By August the Cold Harbor and Petersburg pictures were on display at the Brady gallery in New York City, and *Harper's Weekly* reported that Brady had returned from the army in Virginia with new images of the war.[38] And again it was the image of Brady himself in the photographs that fixed the public perception of war photography.

And he was paying a heavy price for it, too—running his business into the ground to pay for his operators in the field. To raise cash, he sold a half share of his Washington gallery to James Gibson, who was then the manager, for $10,000.[39] Like Grant, Brady seemed to be willing to risk it all.

FIGURE 59

FIGURE 59

Gen. Burnside (reading newspaper) with Mathew B. Brady at Cold Harbor, Va. Mathew Brady. June 11 or 12, 1864. Stereograph. Library of Congress.

FIGURE 60

Petersburg, Va.: Artillery battery. Mathew Brady. June 21, 1864. National Archives.

Brady is standing by the wheel of the artillery piece. Over the years this picture was often titled Brady Under Fire, *giving further emphasis to the photographer's presence on the front lines. But it is obvious that this artillery battery is not in action or under fire: For the photograph to have this clarity, the men had to have been posed standing perfectly still for several seconds at least—much too long to wait motionless during a fight, and a noncombatant would not have been allowed on the scene during a bombardment. But the persistence of the misleading title points out how many people believe Brady to have been on the scene of every battle.*

FIGURE 61

Gen. Grant in front of his tent, Cold Harbor, Va. Mathew Brady. June 11 or 12, 1864. National Archives.

FIGURE 60

FIGURE 61

22.

BALLOTS AND BULLETS

With September came the evacuation of Atlanta, Georgia, by the Confederates. Sherman's army rolled on through, while the siege of Petersburg continued, but meanwhile, the government of the people, by the people, for the people, was carrying on business as usual, even in the midst of civil war. The year 1864 was a presidential election year, and Lincoln was running for a second term in the White House—and of all people, he was running against General McClellan. General *McClellan,* who was running to stop the war and let the Confederacy alone. For McClellan to oust Lincoln would be the clearest possible message that the Union disapproved of how the president had been carrying out the war, and of the war itself.

Lincoln's main concern was how the soldiers voted. If he could get the army to back him and not Little Mac, he would have his answer on how the war was going.[40] In October many regiments cast absentee ballots with election commissioners on hand to make sure that anyone who wanted to vote had the chance to do so. Late in the month a regiment of Pennsylvania volunteers camped on the White House grounds held their balloting: Tad Lincoln ran to his father's office to tell the president to look out the window and watch the soldiers vote.[41]

That there could even be a presidential election in the midst of a civil war was seen as a great victory for the republic, and it proved to the voters that this truly was a remarkable thing, this government of theirs, and worth defending. November 8 saw Lincoln reelected, sweeping the soldier vote by a huge majority.[42]

The war would continue until the rebellion was put down.

The siege of Petersburg continued.

FIGURE 62
Crowds at Lincoln's second inauguration. March 4, 1865. Library of Congress.

23.

AND THEN...?

As 1865 began, it was no longer a question of whether the war would end and who would win it, but how soon the Union would triumph. With General Sherman's army camped outside Savannah, Georgia, Grant's army sitting between Petersburg and Richmond, and rebel forces in Tennessee reduced almost to nothing, the numbers were finally, *finally* catching up with General Lee. The Confederacy's days were truly numbered. Charleston, where the rebellion had begun, was evacuated in the middle of February—and Fort Sumter with it.

Washington was swarming with soldiers. The city was a mass of hospitals and army camps, and men on furlough made the city a throng of blue uniforms. The bridges across the Potomac saw a steady stream of soldiers, with guards examining passes as the late winter evenings closed in.[43] In the first days of March an immense drove of two thousand mules was driven by wranglers up K Street; a deluge of rain and hail poured onto the city, sluicing the mud and manure from choked gutters. There was a sense that this would all be over soon.

And then what would happen? How would the rebel states be treated? As prodigal sons, welcomed home with open arms? Or punished for disobedience? It could be said that they'd already been punished—pummeled and pounded, their farms and towns in smoking ruins, their men crippled or in the grave. President Lincoln made his wishes perfectly clear. "With malice toward none; with charity for all; with firmness in the right, as God gives us to see the right, let us strive on to finish the work we are in: to bind up the nation's wounds; to care for him who shall have borne the battle, and for his widow and his orphan."[44]

But before the country worked for a lasting peace, it had to finish this work. The end of March brought the beginning of the end, the campaign to squeeze Lee into a corner. Rain poured steadily. The government of the Confederacy evacuated Richmond, and photographers swarmed in, taking views all over the rebel capital. A Richmond newspaper reported, "M. B. Brady, Esq., the celebrated Photographist of New York City, and Washington, is in

Richmond with a full corps of artists, apparatus and material."[45]

Lee's army was spread unbearably thin, retreating westward with Union forces closing in from all sides. It was pointless to continue. "The result of the last week must convince you of the hopelessness of further resistance on the part of the Army of Northern Virginia in this struggle,"[46] Grant wrote to Lee on April 7. "I feel that it is so, and regard it as my duty to shift from myself the responsibility of any further effusion of blood, by asking of you the surrender of that portion of the C.S. Army known as the Army of Northern Virginia."

So that was the end of it, then. Lee agreed to meet Grant and make it formal. On April 9 Lee arrived at the McLean house—an elegant, refined gentleman. Grant, in working clothes and without a sword, met him inside to get the business over with. They went over the terms of the surrender: Men with horses would be allowed to keep them, to go home and get on with spring planting. Normal life, or some imitation of it, would have to resume.

When Lee returned to his men, he told them, "I have done for you all that it was in my power to do. You have all done your duty. Leave the result to God. Go to your homes and resume your occupations. Obey the laws and become as good citizens as you were soldiers." His soldiers cried as he rode past.[47] Union artillerymen began firing in celebration, only to be scolded by Grant not to humiliate their fellow countrymen; the soldiers of the South were rebels no more but Americans.[48] And at the same time, Lincoln was visiting soldiers in a hospital. "The men not only reverence and admire Mr. Lincoln, but they love him. May God bless him, and spare his life to us for many years," wrote one of them in his diary that evening.[49] Lee, Grant, and Lincoln: three men who had done all they could do, to the best of their abilities and in their own ways. Although fighting would continue here and there for a few more weeks, the war was officially over; the Union was preserved, and the South was . . . ruined.

The next day Tad Lincoln asked for a Confederate flag; one was given to him, and he waved it from a window at the White House, while crowds cheered below.[50] Four days later, another flag, this one a Union Stars and Stripes, was raised over Fort Sumter by the Union officer who had had to relinquish the fort four years before, Major—now General—Robert Anderson. It was over. It was over at last.

That night, John Wilkes Booth murdered the president.

FIGURE 63

FIGURE 64

FIGURE 65

FIGURE 66

Petersburg, Va.: Union troops in trenches before battle. A. F. Russell. National Archives.

Alternately identified as soldiers on the west bank of Rappahannock River before May 1863 Chancellorsville engagement.

24.

FIXED

"General Lee and staff—or rather those who accompanied him to Richmond—were yesterday photographed in a group by Mr. Brady of New York. Six different sittings were taken of General Lee, each in a different posture, and all were pronounced admirable pictures," reported a Richmond newspaper on April 21.[51] Brady had traded on his reputation to get a portrait of Lee—a gentleman of Virginia, no longer an officer of the feared Army of Northern Virginia; a somber man in retirement, his gaze fixed somewhere beyond the camera, fixed on what might have been. Brady had dallied at Richmond, and so was on hand when Lee returned from the surrender at Appomattox. It is unlikely that anyone else could have gotten permission to make such a portrait.[52] Everything the South had prided itself on was embodied in this man. And he had surrendered.

The South was reeling from its defeat, and reeling too (along with the North) from the death of Abraham Lincoln. He had begun putting forth his plans for what would be called Reconstruction; his inaugural speech had spoken of reconciliation, reunion. The whole city of Washington had been draped in funeral black; citizens and soldiers of the United States stood numb and quiet, all the joy drained from their victory with their terrible loss. Now who could say how the damage of the Civil War would be undone, how the broken country would be fixed? Would it? Could it? And what of the country's great sin of slavery? Slavery had been abolished, but the wound was still raw and painful—could that ever be healed?

The men and events of the war were already passing into myth, the battlefields becoming farmland again, where the plow unearthed and reburied the bones and the muskets of fallen soldiers. The photographic images made during the war fixed the men and those places in time: These soldiers would forever be sitting in front of their tent; these officers would forever be standing by a tree; Lincoln would forever gaze at them from deep-set eyes. And there they would be left, fixed in history and memory while the country moved on.

It would be Brady's name attached to those images and to those memories. The photographer who had staked everything he had on documenting the war enlisted the support of every influential friend to help him create a permanent display of the pictures at government expense. "It is because man is essentially a historical creature; because he is bound by mysterious ties of interest and affection to the past; because he 'looks before and after,' that we desire to see the large and valuable collection of Mr. Brady . . . fitly placed for permanent preservation and exhibition," proclaimed the press.[53]

"It is highly fortunate that a photographer of such undaunted enterprise as Mr. Brady has exerted himself so untiringly and with such success in the work of permanently fixing for future generations the fleeting scenes of our great civil war," wrote the *Evening Post* of New York. "The military camps, fortifications, reviews, siege trains—the farmhouses, plantations and famous buildings of the South—the groups of prominent army and naval officers of the field and on the decks of our war vessels—the horrors of war, and its lighter aspects as seen around the bivouac fires, are all portrayed exactly as they were, and as no pen could describe them."[54]

But in fact it never happened. Perhaps the memories and the wounds were still too fresh. Perhaps the country did not wish to be reminded of how it had hurt itself. Or perhaps the reproductions of his Photo

by Brady images—in the newspapers and magazines, in the *cartes de visite* sold by the hundreds—were so plentiful that the public had seen enough already. But Brady was not able to convince the government to buy the complete set of his pictures, and the negatives were dispersed. The portrait of the war would never be seen as a whole. Mathew Brady had fixed himself into America's memory, however, as the man who had shown the country that picture. The shared memory that he was so instrumental in creating became part of the glue that turned America back into one nation, bound up its wounds, and made it whole.

PICTURE THIS

July 3, 1913: Gettysburg, Pennsylvania. There is the wall where, fifty years before, General Pickett led his men toward the moment the tide turned. Gray-bearded men, veterans of the Army of Northern Virginia, are marching uphill toward that wall, while gray-bearded veterans of the Army of the Potomac march down. In the tall grass insects whir and hum. Birds wheel overhead. The sun is hot. On either side the veterans reach the wall at the same time; they reach out across the divide; they shake hands.

FIGURE 67

NOTES

PREPARATION OF THE PLATE

1. Mary Panzer. *Mathew Brady and the Image of History,* p. 11.
2. Mary Panzer. op. cit., p. 216.
3. Ibid., p. 210.
4. Ibid., p. 44.
5. Ibid., p. 48.
6. Ibid., p. 44.
7. James David Horan. *Mathew Brady, Historian with a Camera,* p. 25.
8. Mark D. Katz. *Witness to an Era,* p. 14.
9. Panzer. op. cit., pp. 55-56.
10. Ibid.
11. Roy Meredith. *Mathew Brady's Portrait of an Era,* p. 65.
12. Katz, op. cit., p. 7.
13. Horan, op. cit., p. 25.
14. George Sullivan. *Picturing Lincoln,* p. 26.
15. Ibid.
16. William C. Davis. *Lincoln's Men,* p. 19.
17. Harold Holzer. *Witness to War,* p. 16.

EXPOSURE

1. Katz, op. cit., p. 19.
2. Ibid., p. 18.
3. Meredith, op. cit., p. 105.
4. Horan, op. cit., p. 46.
5. Panzer, op. cit., p. xix.
6. E. B. Long with Barbara Long. *The Civil War Day by Day,* p. 35.
7. George Sullivan. *Portraits of War,* p. 25.
8. George Sullivan. *Picturing Lincoln,* p. 36.
9. Ibid., p. 38.
10. Long, op. cit., p. 46.
11. Long, op. cit., p. 49.
12. Bruce Catton. *This Hallowed Ground,* p. 20.
13. Emmy E. Werner. *Reluctant Witnesses,* p. 8.
14. Bell Irwin Wiley. *The Life of Billy Yank,* p. 18.
15. Davis, op. cit., p. 43.
16. Holzer, op. cit., 29.
17. Davis, op. cit., p. 29.
18. Ibid., p. 59.
19. Walt Whitman. *The Sacrificial Years,* p. 89.
20. Roy Meredith. *Mr. Lincoln's Camera Man,* p. 88.
21. Horan, op. cit., p. 38.
22. Meredith, *Mr. Lincoln's Camera Man,* p. 90.
23. Katz, op. cit., p. 19.
24. Horan, op. cit., p. 41.
25. William Frassanito. *Gettysburg,* p. 30.
26. Katz, op. cit., p. 73.
27. Panzer, op. cit., p. 108.
28. Katz, op. cit., p. 25.
29. Holzer, op. cit., p. 34.
30. Earl J. Hess. *The Union Soldier in Battle,* p. 76.
31. Horan, op. cit., p. 39.
32. Elizabeth Blair Lee. *Wartime Washington,* p. 65.
33. Stephen W. Sears. *To the Gates of Richmond,* p. 3.
34. Davis, op. cit., p. 53.
35. Catton, op. cit., p. 86.
36. Long, op. cit., p. 145.
37. Richard Wheeler. *Voices of the Civil War,* p. 56.
38. Robert Knox Sneden. *Eye of the Storm,* p. 5.
39. Wiley, op. cit., p. 128.
40. Time-Life Books. *Soldier Life,* p. 28.
41. Meredith, *Mr. Lincoln's Camera Man,* p. 92.
42. Katz, op. cit., p. 28.
43. Sneden, op. cit., p. 5.
44. Ibid., p. 15.
45. Wiley, op. cit., p. 233.
46. Ibid., p. 49.
47. Wilbur Fisk. *Hard Marching Every Day,* p. 73.
48. Time-Life, op. cit., p. 27.
49. Long, op. cit., p. 164.
50. Long, op. cit., p. 166.
51. Davis, op. cit., p. 62.
52. Sneden, op. cit., p. 20.
53. Davis, op. cit., p. 63.
54. Sneden, op. cit., p. 26.
55. Fisk, op. cit., p. 15.
56. Lee, op. cit., p. 114.
57. Sears, op. cit., p. 24.
58. Sneden, op. cit., p. 28.
59. Robert Knox Sneden. *Images from the Storm,* p. 29.
60. Wiley, op. cit., p. 335.
61. Sears, op. cit., p. 24.
62. Sneden. *Images from the Storm,* p. 35.
63. Wheeler, op. cit., p. 121.
64. Fisk, op. cit., p. 19.
65. Sneden. *Eye of the Storm,* pp. 39-40.
66. Davis, op. cit., p. 48.
67. Fisk, op. cit., p. 365.
68. Wiley, op. cit., p. 236.
69. Theodore Ayrault Dodge. *On Campaign with the Army of the Potomac,* p. 41.
70. Sneden. *Eye of the Storm,* p. 50.
71. Wheeler, op. cit., p. 119.
72. Catton, op. cit., p. 134.
73. Dodge, op. cit., p. 29.
74. Wheeler, op. cit., p. 149.
75. Sneden. *Eye of the Storm,* p. 73.
76. Katz, op. cit., p. 31.
77. Panzer, op. cit., p. 110.
78. Horan, op. cit., p. 39.
79. Davis, op. cit., p. 67.
80. Meredith. *Mr. Lincoln's Camera Man,* p. 117.

DEVELOPING THE IMAGE

1. Wheeler, op. cit., p. 178.
2. Hess, op. cit., p. 133.
3. Catton, op. cit., p. 64.
4. Long, op. cit., p. 265.
5. Wheeler, op. cit., p. 193.
6. William A. Frassanito. *Antietam*, p. 42.
7. Hess, op. cit., p. 47.
8. Werner, op. cit., p. 30.
9. Wheeler, op. cit., p. 187.
10. Catton, op. cit., p. 168.
11. Wheeler, op. cit., p. 191.
12. Whitman, op. cit., p. 64.
13. Wiley, op. cit., p. 81.
14. Sneden. *Eye of the Storm*, p. 75.
15. Catton, op. cit., p. 169.
16. Wheeler, op. cit., p. 194.
17. Frassanito. *Antietam*, p. 53.
18. Ibid., pp. 15-16.
19. Wheeler, op. cit., p. 198.
20. Catton, op. cit., p. 171.
21. Long, op. cit., p. 275.
22. Wheeler, op. cit., p. 200.
23. Holzer, op. cit., p. 86.
24. Ibid., p. 80.
25. Long, op. cit., pp. 284–285.
26. Katz, op. cit., p. 28.
27. Ibid., p. 50.
28. Ibid., p. 47.
29. Sullivan. *Portraits of War*, p. 47.
30. Panzer, op. cit., p. xix.
31. Wheeler, op. cit., p. 208.
32. Holzer, op. cit., p. 88.
33. Catton, op. cit., p. 187.
34. Werner, op. cit., p. 33.
35. Long, op. cit., p. 296.
36. Whitman, op. cit., p. 26.
37. Ibid., p. 18.
38. Ibid., p. 20.
39. *Soldier Life*, p. 31.
40. Holzer, op. cit., p. 101.
41. *Soldier Life*, p. 89.
42. Catton, op. cit., p. 204.
43. Panzer, op. cit., p. 187.
44. *Soldier Life*, p. 40.
45. Fisk, op. cit., p. 58.
46. Long, op. cit., p. 335.
47. Catton, op. cit., p. 239.
48. Joseph Hooker to Abraham Lincoln, May 3, 1863 (Telegram reporting battle at Chancellorsville). Abraham Lincoln Papers at the Library of Congress. Transcribed and Annotated by the Lincoln Studies Center, Knox College, Galesburg, Illinois.
49. Werner, op. cit., p. 56.
50. Holzer, op. cit., p. 115.
51. Hess, op. cit., p. 132.
52. Long, op. cit., p. 364.
53. Meredith. *Lincoln's Camera Man*, p. 151.
54. Catton, op. cit., p. 245.
55. Fisk, op. cit., p. 107.
56. Werner, op. cit., p. 60.
57. Ibid., p. 65.
58. Hess, op. cit., p. 17.
59. Fisk, op. cit., p. 116.
60. Lee, op. cit., p. 281.
61. Frassanito. *Gettysburg,* pp. 24–26.
62. Catton, op. cit., p. 255.
63. Holzer, op. cit., p. 122.
64. Ibid., p. 126.
65. Whitman, op. cit., p. 49.
66. Lee, op. cit., p. 283.
67. Werner, op. cit., p.73.
68. Meredith. *Mr. Lincoln's Camera Man,* p. 154.
69. Frassanito. *Gettysburg,* p. 30.
70. Ibid., p. 31.

FIXING THE IMAGE

1. Frassanito. *Gettysburg,* p. 38.
2. Katz, op. cit., p. 69.
3. Horan, op. cit., p. 53.
4. Katz, op. cit., p. 85.
5. Frassanito. *Gettysburg,* p. 233.
6. Catton, op. cit., p. 265.
7. Davis, op. cit., p. 160.
8. Whitman, op. cit., p. 57.
9. Ibid., p. 66.
10. Long, op. cit., p. 398.
11. Catton, op. cit., p. 314.
12. Whitman, op. cit., p. 88.
13. Lee, op. cit., p. 355.
14. Meredith, *Mr. Lincoln's Camera Man,* p. 162.
15. Ibid.
16. Long, op. cit., p. 476.
17. Fisk, op. cit., p. 204.
18. Catton, op. cit., p. 316.
19. Ibid., pp. 317-318.
20. Ibid., p. 321.
21. Lee, op. cit., p. 379.
22. Holzer, op. cit., p. 147.
23. Ibid., p. 145.
24. Catton, op. cit., p. 322.
25. Wiley, op. cit., p. 75.
26. Catton, op., cit., p. 323.
27. Daniel Chisolm. *The Civil War Notebook of Daniel Chisolm,* p. 13.
28. Catton, op. cit., p. 327.
29. Holzer, op. cit., p. 146.
30. Ibid., p. 152.
31. Long, op. cit., p. 500.
32. Lee, op. cit., p. 381.
33. Long, op. cit., p. 500.
34. Catton, op. cit., p. 207.
35. Lee, op. cit., p. 385.
36. William A. Frassanito. *Grant and Lee,* p. 281.
37. Chisolm, op. cit., p. 24.
38. Panzer, op. cit., p. xx.
39. Ibid.
40. Davis, op. cit., p. 193.
41. Ibid., p. 217.
42. Holzer, op. cit., p. 139.
43. Whitman, op. cit., p. 120.
44. Long, op. cit., p. 647.
45. www.civilwarrichmond.com
46. Long, op. cit., p. 668.
47. Long, op. cit., p. 671.
48. Catton, op. cit., p. 389.
49. Fisk, op. cit., p. 323.
50. Werner, op. cit., p. 139.
51. www.civilwarrichmond.com
52. Frassanito, *Grant and Lee,* p. 416.
53. Panzer, op. cit., p. 116.
54. Ibid., p. 221.

BIBLIOGRAPHY

Catton, Bruce. *This Hallowed Ground: The Story of the Union Side of the Civil War.* Garden City, N. Y.: Doubleday, 1956.

Chisholm, Daniel. *The Civil War Notebook of Daniel Chisholm: A Chronicle of Daily Life in the Union Army, 1864-1865.* Edited by W. Springer Menge and J. August Shimrak. New York: Orion Books, 1989.

Civil War Richmond Web site: www.civilwarrichmond.com.

Davis, William C. *Lincoln's Men: How President Lincoln Became Father to an Army and a Nation.* New York: Free Press, 1999.

Dodge, Theodore Ayrault. *On Campaign with the Army of the Potomac: The Civil War Journal of Theodore Ayrault Dodge.* Edited by Stephen W. Sears. New York: Cooper Square Press, 2001.

Fisk, Wilbur. *Hard Marching Every Day: The Civil War Letters of Private Wilbur Fisk, 1861-1865.* Edited by Emil and Ruth Rosenblatt. Anti-rebel Series. Lawrence, Kan.: University Press of Kansas, 1992.

Frassanito, William A. *Antietam: The Photographic Legacy of America's Bloodiest Day.* New York: Scribner's, 1978.

———. *Gettysburg: A Journey in Time.* New York, Scribner's, 1975.

———. *Grant and Lee: The Virginia Campaigns, 1864-1865.* New York: Scribner's, 1983.

Hess, Earl J. *The Union Soldier in Battle: Enduring the Ordeal of Combat.* Lawrence, Kan.: University Press of Kansas, 1997.

Holzer, Harold. *Witness to War: The Civil War, 1861-1865.* New York: Berkley Pub., 1996.

Horan, James David. *Mathew Brady, Historian with a Camera.* Picture collation by Gertrude Horan. New York: Crown Publishers, 1955.

Katz, D. Mark. *Witness to an Era: The Life and Photographs of Alexander Gardner: The Civil War, Lincoln, and the West.* New York: Viking, 1991.

Lee, Elizabeth Blair. *Wartime Washington: The Civil War Letters of Elizabeth Blair Lee.* Edited by Virginia Jeans Laas. Urbana, Ill.: University of Illinois Press, 1991.

Lincoln Papers. Library of Congress.

Long, E. B. (Everette Beach) with Barbara Long. *The Civil War Day by Day: An Almanac, 1861-1865.* Garden City, N.Y.: Doubleday, 1971.

Meredith, Roy. *Mathew Brady's Portrait of an Era.* New York: Norton, 1982.

———. *Mr. Lincoln's Cameraman, Mathew B. Brady.* New York: Scribner's, 1946.

Panzer, Mary. *Mathew Brady and the Image of History*. Washington, D.C.: Smithsonian Institution Press for the National Portrait Gallery, 1997.

Sears, Stephen W. *To the Gates of Richmond: The Peninsula Campaign*. New York: Ticknor & Fields, 1992.

Sneden, Robert Knox. *Eye of the Storm: A Civil War*. Edited by Charles F. Bryan Jr., and Nelson D. Lankford. New York: Free Press, 2000.

———. *Images from the Storm: 300 Civil War Images*. Edited by Charles F. Bryan Jr., James C. Kelly, and Nelson D. Lankford. New York: Free Press, 2001.

Soldier Life. By the editors of Time-Life Books. Alexandria, Va.: Voices of the Civil War Series, Time-Life Books, 1996.

Sullivan, George. *Picturing Lincoln: Famous Photographs That Popularized the President*. New York: Clarion Books, 2000.

Sullivan, George. *Portraits of War: Civil War Photographers and Their Work*. Brookfield, Conn.: Twenty-First Century Books, 1998.

Werner, Emmy E. *Reluctant Witnesses: Children's Voices from the Civil War*. Boulder, Colo.: Westview Press, 1998.

Wheeler, Richard. *Voices of the Civil War*. New York: Meridian, 1976.

Whitman, Walt. *The Sacrificial Years: A Chronicle of Walt Whitman's Experiences in the Civil War*. Edited by John Harmon McElroy. Boston: David R. Godine, 1999.

Wiley, Bell Irvin. *The Life of Billy Yank, the Common Soldier of the Union*. Indianapolis, Ind.: Bobbs-Merrill, 1952.

PICTURE CREDITS

A word of caution: Photographic historians have debated many of these photographs—dates, places, and photographers have been disputed in many cases. The following catalog information is as it exists in the archives where the images are stored, but is not warranted to be unfailingly accurate simply because the source claims it to be so....

PREPARATION OF THE PLATE

Figure 1 Self-portrait. Mathew B. Brady. National Archives photo no. 111-B-1074.

Figure 2 Portrait of Thomas Cole. National Portrait Gallery, Smithsonian Institution/Art Resource, NY.

Figure 3 Portrait of Thaddeus Hyatt. Fogg Museum of Art, Harvard University Art Museums, on loan from the Historical Photographs and Special Visual Collections Department, Fine Arts Library, Harvard College Library, Bequest of Evert Jansen Wendell, acquisition no. 119.1976.116.

Figure 4 "Landsdowne": Portrait of George Washington by Gilbert Stuart, 1796. Acquired as a gift to the nation through the generosity of the Donald W. Reynolds Foundation. National Portrait Gallery, Smithsonian Institution/Art Resource, NY.

Figure 5 "Cooper Union Portrait" of Abraham Lincoln by Mathew B. Brady. Library of Congress, Prints & Photographs Division, LC-USZ62-5803.

EXPOSURE

Figure 6 *Carte de visite:* Unidentified Union officer, Brady's National Photographic Galleries. Library of Congress, Prints & Photographs Division, LC-USZ62-119421.

Figure 7 Mrs. Abraham Lincoln. Library of Congress, Prints & Photographs Division, LC-DIG-cwpbh-01022.

Figure 8 Inauguration of President Lincoln at U.S. Capitol. March 4, 1861. Library of Congress, Manuscript Division, LC-USZ62-48564.

Figure 9 Zouaves, 9th N.Y. Volunteer Infantry. National Archives photo no. 111-B-5886.

Figure 10 Professor Thaddeus Lowe's balloon gas generators. The U.S. Capitol in background. National Archives photo no. 16-AD-2.

Figure 11 Fair Oaks, Va., vicinity. Gen. George Stoneman and staff. James Gibson. June 1862. Library of Congress, Prints & Photographs Division, LC-B8171-0436 DLC.

Figure 12 Manassas, Va. "Our photographer at Manassas." Timothy O'Sullivan. July 4, 1862. Library of Congress, Prints & Photographs Division, LC-B8184-651 DLC.

Figure 13 Bull Run, Va., View of the battlefield. Library of Congress, Prints & Photographs Division, LC–B8171–1046 DLC.

Figure 14 Gen. George B. McClellan. Mathew Brady. c. 1861. Library of Congress, Prints & Photographs Division, LC–USZ62–12154.

Figure 15 Brady returned from Bull Run, July 22, 1861. Library of Congress, Prints & Photographs Division, LC–BH827701–550–DLC.

Figure 16 Zouave ambulance crew demonstrating removal of wounded soldiers from the field. Library of Congress, Prints & Photographs Division, LC–DIG–cwpb–04095 DLC.

Figure 17 Rappahannock River, Va. Fugitive African Americans fording the Rappahannock. Timothy O'Sullivan. August 1862. Library of Congress, Prints & Photographs Division, LC– B8171–0518 DLC.

Figure 18 Landing, James River, National Archives photo no. 111–B–428.

Figure 19 Cumberland Landing, Va., Group of "contrabands" at Foller's house. James Gibson. May 14, 1862. Library of Congress, Prints & Photographs Division, LC–B8171–0383 DLC.

Figure 20 Fair Oaks, Va., vicinity. Battery M., 2d U.S. Artillery, commanded by Capt. Henry Benson. James Gibson. June 1862. Library of Congress, Prints & Photographs Division, LC–B8171–0433 DLC.

Figure 21 Fair Oaks, Va. Prof. Thaddeus S. Lowe observing the battle from his balloon, *Intrepid*. May 31, 1862. Library of Congress, Prints & Photographs Division, LC–B8171–2348 DLC.

Figure 22 The Peninsula, Va. Lt. George A. Custer with dog. Library of Congress, Prints & Photographs Division, LC–DIG–cwpb–01553 DLC.

Figure 23 Savage Station, Va., Field hospital after the battle of June 27. James Gibson. June 30, 1862. Library of Congress, Prints & Photographs Division, LC–B8171–0491 DLC.

Figure 24 Chickahominy River, Va., Military bridge built by the 15th N.Y. Volunteers under Col. John McL. Murphy. James Gibson. Library of Congress, Prints & Photographs Division, LC–B8171–0489 DLC.

Figure 25 Bealeton, Va. Group at tent and wagon of the *New York Herald*. Timothy O'Sullivan. August 1863. Library of Congress, Prints & Photographs Division, LC–B8171–7235 DLC.

Figure 26 Gen. George B. McClellan and staff of eight. Mathew Brady Studio. National Archives photo no. 111–B–498.

Figure 27 Virginia. Newspaper vendor and cart in camp. Alexander Gardner. November 1863. Library of Congress, Prints & Photographs Division, LC–B8171–0617 DLC.

DEVELOPING THE IMAGE

Figure 28 Washington D.C., The Long Bridge over the Potomac seen from the city. May 1865. Library of Congress, Prints & Photographs Division, LC-DIG-cwpb-04247 DLC.

Figure 29 Antietam, Md. Antietam Bridge on the Sharpsburg–Boonboro Turnpike. Alexander Gardner. September 1862. Library of Congress, Prints & Photographs Division LC-DIG-cwpb-03889.

Figure 30 Dunker Church, on the battlefield of Antietam. Stereograph by Alexander Gardner. 1862. "Photographic Incidents of the War" 573. New-York Historical Society #PR 065-788-24, digital i.d. number ad 18024.

Figure 31 The sunken road at Antietam. Stereograph by Alexander Gardner, 1862. "Photographic History, The War for the Union" 553. New-York Historical Society #PR 065-788-41, digital i.d. number ad 18041.

Figure 32 Horse of Confederate colonel, both killed at the Battle of Antietam. Stereograph by Alexander Gardner. 1862. Brady's Album Gallery 558. New-York Historical Society #PR 065-788-10, digital i.d. number ad 18010.

Figure 33 Antietam, Md. Confederate dead by a fence on the Hagerstown road. Alexander Gardner. September 1862. Library of Congress, Prints & Photographs Division, LC-B8171-0560 DLC.

Figure 34 Antietam, Md. Bodies of Confederate dead gathered for burial. Alexander Gardner. September 1862. Library of Congress, Prints & Photographs Division, LC-B8171-0557 DLC.

Figure 35 Antietam, Md. President Lincoln with Gen. George B. McClellan and group of officers. Alexander Gardner. October 3, 1862. Library of Congress, Prints & Photographs Division, LC-DIG-cwpb-04352.

Figure 36 Antietam, Md. President Lincoln and Gen. George B. McClellan in the general's tent. Alexander Gardner. October 3, 1862. Library of Congress, Prints & Photographs Division, LC-B8171-7948 DLC.

Figure 37 Fredericksburg from the river, Mathew Brady Studio. National Archives photo no. 111-B-438.

Figure 38 Fredericksburg, Va. View of town from east bank of the Rappahannock. Timothy O'Sullivan. March 1863. Library of Congress, Prints & Photographs Division, LC-DIG-cwpb-04325.

Figure 39 Carver Hospital, Washington, D.C. Interior view. Mathew Brady Studio. National Archives photo no. 111-B-173.

Figure 40 Mr. and Mrs. Gen. Tom Thumb, Commodore Nutt, and Miss Minnie Warren. Stereograph by Mathew B. Brady. George Eastman House 83:0045:0001.

Figure 41 Camp scene showing winter huts and corduroy roads. Mathew Brady Studio. National Archives photo no. 111-B-223.

Figure 42 Confederate dead behind a stone wall at Marye's Heights. National Archives photo no. 111-B-514.

Figure 43 Marye's Heights, Fredericksburg, Va. May 3, 1863. Mathew Brady Studio. National Archives photo no. 111-B-74.

Figure 44 Incidents of the war: A harvest of death, Gettysburg, July 1863. Timothy O'Sullivan. Library of Congress, Prints & Photographs Division, LC-B8184-7964-A DLC.

Figure 45 Gettysburg, Pa. Dead Confederate soldier in Devil's Den. (Also known as "The Home of a Rebel Sharpshooter, Gettysburg.") Alexander Gardner. Library of Congress, Prints & Photographs Division, LC-B8171-7942 DLC.

Figure 46 View at Losser's [Trostle's] Barn, where the 9th Massachusetts battery was cut up. Stereograph by Timothy H. O'Sullivan. 1863. "Photographic Incidents of the War" 266. New-York Historical Society. #PR 065-793-43, digital i.d. number ad 23043.

FIXING THE IMAGE

Figure 47 Cemetery gate, Gettysburgh (Evergreen Cemetery). Stereograph, Brady & Co., Washington, D.C., "Photographic History, The War for the Union, War Views" 2388. New-York Historical Society #PR 065-793-6, digital i.d. number ad 23006.

Figure 48 Part of Gettysburg Battlefield. Mathew Brady Studio. National Archives photo no. 111-B-127.

Figure 49 Gettysburg, Pa. Three Confederate prisoners. Library of Congress, Prints & Photographs Division, LC-DIG-cwpb-01450.

Figure 50 Smithsonian Institution, Washington, D.C. Mathew Brady Studio. National Archives photo no. 111-B-4964.

Figure 51 Gen. Robert B. Potter and staff of seven, recognized. Capt. Gilbert H. McKibben, Capt. Wright, A.A.G. Also Mr. Brady, photographer. Mathew Brady Studio. National Archives photo no. 111-B-44.

Figure 52 Gettysburg, Pa. Crowds at the dedication of the battlefield cemetery. November 19, 1863. Library of Congress, Prints & Photographs Division, LC-DIG-cwpb-00651 DLC.

Figure 53 Brandy Station, Va., vicinity. Large wagon park. Timothy O'Sullivan. May 1864. Library of Congress, Prints & Photographs Division, LC-B-8171-7268 DLC.

Figure 54 Ulysses S. Grant. Mathew Brady Studio. National Archives photo no. 200-CA-38.

Figure 55 The Wilderness, near Chancellorsville, Va. Mathew Brady Studio. National Archives photo no. 111-B-29.

Figure 56 Spotsylvania Court House, Va., vicinity. Burial of soldier by Mrs. Alsop's house, near which Ewell's Corps attacked the Federal right on May 19, 1864. Timothy O'Sullivan. Library of Congress, Prints & Photographs Division, LC-B8171-0721 DLC.

Figure 57 View of North Anna, with railroad bridge in the distance. Stereograph by Timothy H. O'Sullivan. c. 1861–65. "Photographic Incidents of the War" 763. New-York Historical Society #PR-065-810-8 digital i.d. number ad 40008.

Figure 58 Massaponax Church, Va., *Council of War*. Gen. Ulysses S. Grant examining map held by Gen. George G. Meade. Timothy O'Sullivan. Library of Congress, Prints & Photographs Division, LC-DIG-cwpb-0 DLC.

Figure 59 Gen. Ambrose E. Burnside (reading
newspaper) with Mathew B. Brady (nearest
tree) at Army of the Potomac headquarters.
Library of Congress, Prints & Photographs
Division, LC-DIG-cwpb-01702 DLC.

Figure 60 Petersburg, Va., artillery battery.
Brady Under Fire. National Archives photo
no. 111-B-346.

Figure 61 General Grant at Cold Harbor. National
Archives photo no. 111-B-36.

Figure 62 Crowds at Lincoln's second inauguration.
Library of Congress, Prints & Photographs
Division, LC-US762-7812.

Figure 63 McLean House, Appomattox. Timothy
O'Sullivan. April 1865. National Archives
photo no. 165-SB-99.

Figure 64 Cold Harbor, Va. African Americans
collecting bones of soldiers killed in the battle.
John Reekie. April 1865. Library of Congress,
Prints & Photographs Division,
LC-DIG-cwpb-04324 DLC.

Figure 65 Soldiers' graves near the General
Hospital, City Point, Va. Stereograph by
Mathew Brady. c. 1864 to 1865. New-York
Historical Society #PR 065-805-12,
digital i.d. number ad 35012.

Figure 66 In the trenches before Petersburg, Va.
Mathew Brady Studio. National Archives photo
no. 111-B-768.

Figure 67 Robert E. Lee. Mathew B. Brady. 1865.
National Archives photo no. 111-B-1564.

INDEX

Note: Page numbers in ***bold italics*** indicate photographs.